Writing a Children's Book

Writing a Children's Book

How to write for children and get published

3rd Edition

PAMELA CLEAVER

howtobooks

Published by How To Books Ltd,
Spring Hill House, Spring Hill Road,
Begbroke, Oxford OX5 1RX, United Kingdom
Tel: (01865) 375794. Fax: (01865) 379162
email: info@howtobooks.co.uk
www.howtobooks.co.uk

First published 2000
Second edition 2002
Third edition 2004
Reprinted 2004
Reprinted 2005
Reprinted 2007

British Library Cataloguing in Publication Data
A catalogue record for this book is available from the British
Library

ISBN 13: 978 1 85703 925 2

Cover design by Baseline Arts Ltd, Oxford
Produced for How To Books by Deer Park Productions, Tavistock
Typeset by Dorwyn Ltd, Wells, Somerset
Printed and bound by Cromwell Press, Trowbridge, Wiltshire

NOTE: The material contained in this book is set out in good
faith for general guidance and no liability can be accepted
for loss or expense incurred as a result of relying in particular
circumstances on statements made in the book. The laws and
regulations are complex and liable to change, and readers should
check the current position with the relevant authorities before
making personal arrangements.

Contents

Preface   **vii**

1   Preparing to Write   **1**
Writing for children for the right reasons   1
Finding out what children and publishers want   3
The importance of reading   6
Making time to write   8
Cultivating a writer's mind   9
Research your childhood   10
To sum up   10
Exercises   12

2   Deciding What Sort of Story you are Going to Write   14
What sort of books are there?   14
Exercises   26

3   Who is Going to Read your Book?   **28**
Picture books – 0–6 year olds   28
Beginning readers – 5–7 year olds   31
Series books – 7–9 year olds   33
Tween-Agers – 9–12 year olds   34
Teen Fiction – young adult books   35
Exercises   38

4   Plotting and Planning   **39**
How to find plot ideas   39
Keeping track of your ideas   43
How do you develop your ideas?   45
The three parts of a plot   46
What not to write   50
Testing the plot   51
Exercises   53

5   Characters and How to Find Them   **54**
Which comes first, character or plot?   54
Naming your characters   57
Families   58
Getting to know your characters   59

Putting the characters on the page   61
Exercises   66

6   Beginnings   67
How to write your book   67
Developing style   68
Point of view   69
Hooking the reader   70
Exercises   78

7   The Middle of the Book   79
Holding the reader   79
Dialogue   82
Writer's block   86
Exercises   88

8   The End   90
Payoff time   90
Exercises   96

9   Writing a Non-Fiction Book   97
What sort of subjects?   97
Who is the book intended for?   98
Research   99
Approaching a publisher   100
Compiling a book proposal   101
Biographies   103
Step-by-step books   104
Activity books   104
Joke books   104
Exercises   105

10   Revising – Getting it Right   106
Cutting – dumping dead words   106
Choosing a title   111
Preparing your MS   113
Exercises   117

11   Finding a Publisher   118
Sending out your MS   118

Books for further reading   128
Magazines for writers   131
Useful addresses and websites   132
Index   135

Preface

Can creative writing be taught? Many people think not. It is true that talent can't be taught but technique can. There is no one right way to write a children's book but if you are armed with a knowledge of certain techniques that have worked for other writers, you are less likely to make mistakes.

In this book I have set out to answer the many questions I have been asked in eighteen years of teaching Writing for Children and I hope these answers will set you on the road to success.

Please note that throughout the book I use male pronouns for clarity and to avoid clumsiness. If you find this offensive, please feel free to substitute female ones where appropriate.

Grateful thanks to my son Rupert Cleaver who designed the letter headings for the sample letters and arranged the newspaper collage for me.

Finally, I should like to dedicate this book to all my students past and present at the London School of Journalism, Fen Farm, and Writers' News Home Study Division. I have learned from you as I hope you have learned from me and I have loved every minute of it.

Pamela Cleaver

You can contact Pamela at pamelatcuk@yahoo.co.uk if you have any queries about subjects raised in this book. However, Pamela regrets she cannot read your MSS. If you are in need of feedback on your story, why not join a critique group? Go to http://groups.msn.com/TheChildrensBookWritersCafe/cafecritique.msnw where you will find a list of critique groups that currently have openings.

IS THIS YOU?

This book is for people

- who tell their children bedtime stories and would like to see them in print
- who tell stories to the children in their class
- who would like to write, but don't know where to start
- who feel sure they could write if only they knew the tricks of the trade
- who can't afford to take a correspondence course
- who are housebound so can't go to writers' courses
- who belong to a writers' circle
- who are writers looking to expand their range
- who want to communicate with children
- who aren't sure what children want
- who want to recapture the pleasures of childhood
- who don't think they have ever grown up
- who have a vivid imagination
- who love fantasy.

Preparing to Write

'How delightful it must be to write books after one's own taste instead of reading other people's,' said Gwendolyn. 'I would give anything to write a book.'

'And why should you not?' said Mrs Arrowpoint encouragingly. 'You have but to begin as I did. Pen, ink and paper are at everybody's command.'

So wrote George Eliot in *Daniel Deronda*, but it is not quite as easy as that. Before you embark on a children's book, there are several things to consider.

WRITING FOR CHILDREN FOR THE RIGHT REASONS

If you think that writing for children is a soft option, that it will be good practice for writing an adult book, this is not a good reason. A children's book can be more difficult to write than an adult book because you are more restricted by theme, vocabulary and length. When you have only 500 words in which to tell a story, as in a picture book, for instance, every word has to be the right word. Maurice Sendak, who won awards for his picture books, said that sometimes he rewrote the text 300 times to get exactly the right words.

If you think that because your own children or the class you teach love the stories you tell them, it follows that all children everywhere will love them, you could be wrong. A lot of the enjoyment of your children or your class is tied up with them knowing you, the attention you are giving them and the sense of togetherness this creates. The appeal of a children's book needs to be universal.

If you want to write so you can be rich and famous, forget it! Children's writers are far less likely to achieve fame and riches than writers of adult best sellers. However, there is one compensation: children's books have a longer shelf life, so royalties and PLR (Public Lending Right) fill your coffers for a longer time.

If you want to write to recreate the sort of stories you loved when you were a child, this is not the right reason either. Fashions change. Modern stories are sharper, punchier and pacier than those of your childhood, and they deal with a far wider range of subjects.

If, however, you want to write because you have wonderful ideas that excite you, that you want to share with children, this is the right reason for writing a children's book, and you should go ahead and write it.

A golden rule for children's writers

Remember, as award winner Jill Paton Walsh said, 'Only the very best writing that we can produce is good enough for children.'

Will you make a good children's writer?

If you are –

◆ someone with a vivid imagination
◆ someone who remembers the feelings he had in his own childhood
◆ someone who has ideas he wants to share with children –

then the answer is probably 'yes'. BUT if you are –

◆ someone who wants to write to teach or preach
◆ someone who wants to moralise or improve
◆ someone who talks down to children
◆ someone who is not prepared to research
◆ someone who is not prepared to be flexible –

you probably won't make the grade. To be a successful children's writer:

◆ you must be in tune with children of today
◆ you must understand their likes and dislikes
◆ you must have something original to say, something which you can share only with children
◆ you must say it well.

FINDING OUT WHAT CHILDREN AND PUBLISHERS WANT

Children and publishers want the same thing. Children want stories that are fresh and interesting. Publishers want such books because they are what sell.

How do we find out what sort of books these are?

◆ Send for publishers' catalogues or check out their websites. Most publishers list their website in *The Writer's Handbook.* See what sort of subjects they are currently taking.

◆ Visit your local library and make a friend of the children's librarian: she will tell you which books go out most often and which age group likes what.

◆ Get hold of *National Curriculum for English: Books for Key Stages 1 & 2*, and *Books for Key Stages 3 & 4* (Puffin) or *The Waterstone's Guide for the National Curriculum (Key Stages 1 & 2).*

◆ Read, read, and read some more!

Why publishers reject MSS (manuscripts)

In a survey I conducted these were the main reasons publishers gave.

1. Lack of originality

This is the number 1 reason for rejection, so when you are looking for story ideas don't be content with the first thing that occurs to you. Mull it over for several days, think it through. Is it like anything you read in your childhood or that you have read to your children? If the answer is yes, could you give it a twist? If it is about people, would it be more interesting if the characters were animals, and vice versa?

2. Old fashioned material

Are you writing about the world as it is now? Are you really writing for children of today? Many people who want to write for children haven't read any children's books since their own childhood and don't realise how much the genre has changed. They base their writing on the way they and their contemporaries behaved and on the books they read as children.

One way to make sure your material isn't old-fashioned is to read lots of up-to-date children's books before you begin, another is to read your stories to today's children and listen to their comments. Watch children's TV and look at children's comics.

3. Poor writing

♦ Writing for children must be clear and grammatical.
♦ It must be fresh and have zip and zest.
♦ Eschew clichés, try for new similes and metaphors.
♦ A light touch and lots of humour get a thumbs up. Read American books for the 7–11s, they handle this style well.

4. Derivative plots

We are back to lack of originality here. Publishers don't want copies of plots that have been used before – C.S. Lewis fantasies, Alan Garner quests, Tolkien-type creatures not unlike Hobbits, boarding schools for wizards and witches – they want something different. (See 'what not to write' in Chapter 4.) Because there's nothing new under the sun, old ideas can be used but they need a new slant.

5. Likes and dislikes of children are not understood

Publishers frequently complain about this. To get this right, you need to interview children or eavesdrop on their conversations. And while you are investigating, find out what the current expressions are for good and bad – if you are still writing 'super' and 'grotty' you need a lesson in current slang. Find out what makes the child of today tick.

6. 'Not our kind of thing'

Another reason for rejection is sending publishers unsuitable material. This can be avoided by:

- reading their catalogues carefully
- looking in the library or bookshop at the kind of books published by your chosen publisher.

The wrong length is another turn-off. Study the publisher's product carefully, do a word count of a book similar to yours that is for the same age group or the series into which you think your book will fit.

7. The book is boring

This covers nearly all the above reasons.

- If your MS is old fashioned, it will bore the reader.
- If the plot is derivative, it will bore the reader.
- If it doesn't consider the child's likes and dislikes, it will be boring.
- If it points an obvious moral, it will bore the reader's socks off.
- If it is badly written and has no zip, nobody will like it.

Whatever you do, don't be boring!

THE IMPORTANCE OF READING

When American children's author Robert Cormier was asked how he learned his craft he said, 'Reading, reading, reading!

Reading is the most important thing I do besides writing.'

- If you want to write picture books, read as many as you can and analyse them. How many words go to the page? What sort of words? Look at the subjects and make lists of those that appeal to you most. Could you write a different book on that subject? Can you think of a similar sort of subject?

- Read the series books written for the middle range of readers, the 7–11s. Check how many characters there are in the books. How long are they? Note which publishers take slice-of-life books and which take fantasy so that when you write your book you target the right publisher.

- Read books for teenagers, the 11+ group. Notice what sort of subjects they tackle. How many different genres can you spot for this age group? Which is the right genre for you?

- Read children's books out loud. This way you will discover that children's stories, especially those for the younger age groups, are best when they are rhythmical. Reading your own work out loud will show you when you have used an infelicitous word or phrase.

- Read to children whenever you can (your own work as well as other people's) so you can gauge whether the listener's interest is flagging.

- Read book reviews in newspapers and magazines. Although children's books are not as frequently covered as adult books, they do get coverage from time to time and this will give you another clue about what sort of books are being published.

MAKING TIME TO WRITE

'I'm going to write a book when I have the time', is something many people say. But if you really want to write, you will *make* time.

◆ Instead of reading a newspaper in the train on the way to work, could you write, or at least make notes for your book? (Anthony Trollope wrote much of his work on train journeys.)
◆ Instead of watching TV all evening, could you miss a programme and spare an hour to devote to your writing?
◆ Could you write under the dryer at the hairdresser's?
◆ Could you write while you are waiting for a cake to bake?
◆ Could you get up an hour earlier or stay up an hour later to give you writing time?

Thinking time

Thinking time is as important as writing time. American writer Grace Paley said, 'When I'm writing a story, I'm really writing all the time, wholly involved in it. When I'm not writing I'm still thinking.'

Next time you are doing a mechanical job like ironing, cleaning the car, washing the dishes or weeding the garden, use the time constructively, thinking about your story.

◆ Ponder on what is going to happen next.
◆ Get to know your characters better.
◆ Decide how you are going to describe the place where the book is set.

Then when you get to your desk, you won't waste precious writing time working these things out.

CULTIVATING A WRITER'S MIND

Writers need to be observant. Curiosity may have killed the cat, but it is the breath of life for a writer. Keep a notebook with you at all times to note down your observations. A pad of paper at your bedside is useful – sometimes dreams give you usable ideas. (Figure 1 is a sample page from a notebook.)

◆ Get into the habit of watching people and thinking how you would describe them if you were to write about them.
◆ Listen to people talking, especially children. Note what they say and how they say it.
◆ Listen to the slang children use. As mentioned before, the vogue words for 'good' and 'bad' change almost from year to year. Old slang dates a book.
◆ Notice how children react to each other, how they interact with adults.
◆ Go to the children's library and watch how children choose books.
◆ Write down descriptions of places you visit.
◆ Notice the way weather affects the landscape and people's moods.
◆ What sort of sounds can you hear in various places? Contrast town and country sounds.
◆ What can you smell in a new place? Think of a child lying in bed and smelling breakfast cooking. Think of the way a school smells and compare it with an office. Smell is the most evocative of the senses.

◆ Think how you can describe different textures. Contrast the smooth feeling of silk or velvet with the roughness of serge or sacking.

◆ Put quotations in your notebook when something you read strikes you as important; things you disagree with wholeheartedly as well as things with which you agree.

◆ Jot down arresting similies and metaphors – these can act as models when you are looking for substitutes for tired clichés.

◆ Collect nuggets of information on subjects that interest you – you never know when you will want to use them in a book.

RESEARCH YOUR CHILDHOOD

It is important to remember how you felt when you were a child. Although many things were different then – the types of schools, the sweets we ate, family rituals – the feelings and emotions of children do not change. It is useful to write accounts of your childhood and what you did and thought at different ages. As you begin to describe the house you lived in when you were five, all sorts of things you had forgotten will emerge from your memory. This is a treasury you can call upon when you are writing.

TO SUM UP

1. Write because you have a great idea you want to share with children.

2. Only write what interests *you*. If you are bored with what you are writing, you can be sure your readers will lose interest too.

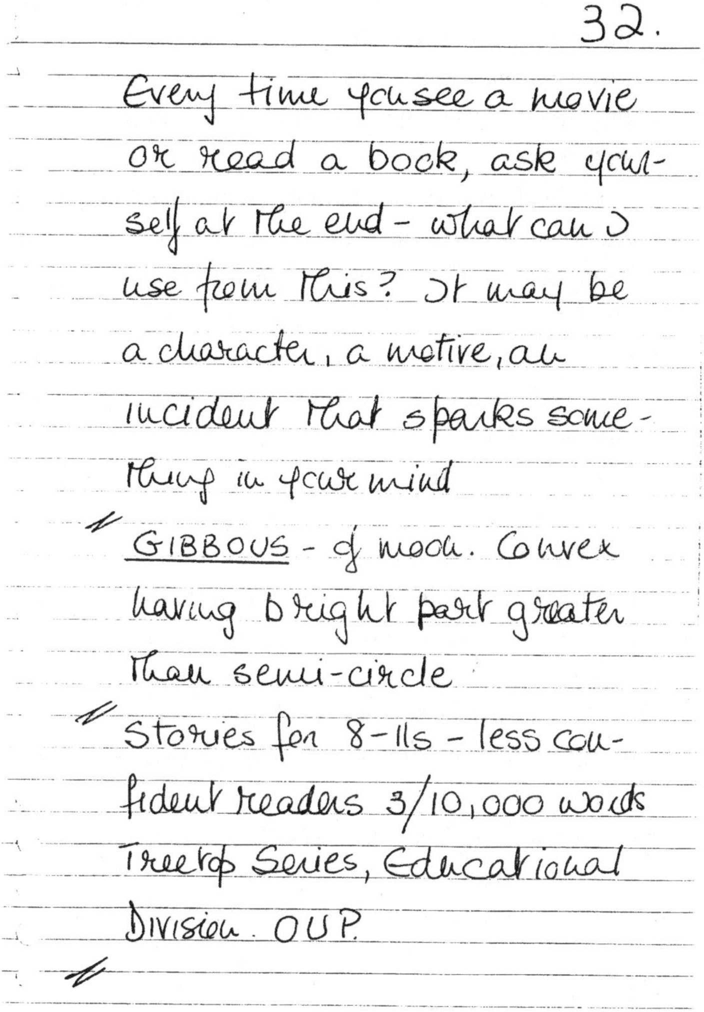

32.

Every time you see a movie
or read a book, ask your-
self at the end - what can I
use from this? It may be
a character, a motive, an
incident that sparks something in your mind

GIBBOUS - of moon. Convex
having bright part greater
than semi-circle

Stories for 8-11s - less con-
fident readers 3/10,000 words
Treetop Series, Educational
Division. OUP.

Fig. 1. Page from a writer's notebook.

3. Read as much as you can, especially current children's books, but don't neglect adult books; you need them to broaden your mind. Enid Blyton said, 'I read every myth and legend I could get hold of. If you want to be a writer you must read, read, read. Try everything, good, bad and indifferent. Sort it out in your own mind, form your taste and find your own bent.'

4. Read good books to see how the author gets the effects you admire: read bad books to see what not to do!

5. Find time to think, find time to write. Try to write every day to keep up momentum. Set yourself manageable targets. For instance, if you write 500 words a day, five days a week, you will have finished a 7,000 word series book in three weeks with time over!

6. Always make a note of an important idea, thought, description or word in your notebook. You may think you will remember, but unless you make a note, you probably won't.

'The horror of that moment,' the White King says in *Alice Through the Looking Glass*, 'I shall never, never forget.'

'You will though,' replies the Queen, 'if you don't make a memorandum of it.'

EXERCISES

1. Write a note to yourself about why you want to write for children. Set yourself a target.

2. Take a picture book, a series book and a young adult book and analyse them as suggested.

3. Write a description of someone you noticed today.

4. Write a description of the house you lived in when you were five years old as it seemed to you then, not as it would appear to an adult.

5. Each day write a thought, an idea or a description in exactly 60 words – not more, not less. This is wonderful practice for tight writing without wasted words – and in cutting, because to begin with you will write too much. If you do only one exercise in this book, this is the one that will prove most useful to you.

(2)

Deciding What Sort of Story you are Going to Write

Just as there are many categories in adult fiction, so there are in children's books. It pays to do your research to find out what sort of books publishers are currently taking, but don't forget what has already been said; you must *want* to write the type of book you choose, otherwise you will bore yourself and your potential readers.

WHAT SORT OF BOOKS ARE THERE?

The fairy tale

This is mostly for younger readers. You can use ingredients such as princesses, enchanters and magic in the traditional way, or modernise the stories using the 'what if' formula. What if the second princess rebelled against her fate? What if the king lost all his money and the princess became a blacksmith to support him? (Both these concepts have been successfully used.)

No need to create the setting here; we all know the landscape of the once-upon-a-time world, familiar to us from our childhood. And we know the rules: if a youth accomplishes three seemingly impossible tasks he wins the princess, and if he ignores a poor old beggar woman he meets on his journey, it will be the worse for him.

An interesting site if you want to create a fairy tale is www.bbc.co.uk/dna/h2g2/A425800. You can select from ten different story lines, add three or four story elements from a selection of fifty, then put your own spin on it.

Imaginary worlds

Stories set entirely in a world invented by the author, such as we find in Tolkien's *The Hobbit* or Philip Pullman's *Northern Lights*. For this category you have to invent the details of your imaginary world. Making a map can be useful. Do not make your imaginary world so different and strange that the reader can't relate to it. There should be echoes of our world: for instance, mix real plants and animals with invented ones as Ursula K. le Guin does in *A Wizard of Earthsea*.

From the real world to another

This is where the story starts in the real world and the characters get into another world as in C.S. Lewis's Narnia books, or Alice going through the looking glass. For this type of book you need to provide:

1. A solid base in reality.
2. An imaginary world.
3. A device or a thin place in reality through which the other world is entered.

As E. Nesbit said:

There is a curtain thin as gossamer, clear as glass, strong as iron that hangs forever between the world of magic and the world as it seems to us to be real. And when once people have found one of the little weak spots in that curtain that are marked by magic rings, and amulets, and the like, almost anything can happen.

Science fiction

Many children who turn up their noses at fantasy enjoy SF, not realising that they both have their roots in folk tales. Many images in SF are folk tales in disguise:

- the hero on his quest becomes an explorer of space
- the monsters he finds become aliens
- the king equates with the captain of the starship *Enterprise*
- the court magician equates with the lieutenant with paranormal powers
- crystal balls, seven league boots and magic wands become closed-circuit TV, jet harnesses and stun guns. Magic rings and amulets are turned into pieces of futuristic gadgetry.

Another influence on SF is history. You can turn the past into the future to make an SF story. As Isaac Asimov wrote:

So success is not a mystery,
Just brush up on your history
　And borrow day by day.
Take an Empire that was Rome
And you'll find it is at home
　In all the starry Milky Way.

With a drive that's hyperspatial

Through the parsecs you will race:
  You'll find that plotting is a breeze
With a tiny bit of cribbin'
From the works of Edward Gibbon
  And that Greek Thucydides.

Role playing

For children who are hooked on computer games, a popular mix of SF and fantasy is used in books where children get inside the machines and suffer the trials that are inbuilt in the games. *The Homeward Bounders* by Diana Wynne Jones and *Sky Maze* by Gillian Rubenstein are good examples: this is a genre that still has plenty of mileage in it.

Robot stories

Robots fascinate children – probably because there seems to be something toy-like about them – look at R2D2 in *Star Wars*. If you write about robots, remember the three laws of robotics laid down by Asimov and almost without exception adhered to by SF writers:

1. A robot may not injure a human being or through inaction allow a human being to come to harm.
2. A robot must obey orders given by a human unless they contravene law 1.
3. A robot must protect its own existence unless this conflicts with laws 1 and 2.

Time-travel and time-slip

Both are popular with children who like the idea of going into the past or future to find out what is different and exotic, and perhaps to reap rewards their foreknowledge might bring. But as John Buchan wrote in *The Gap in the Curtain*:

> Our ignorance of the future has been wisely ordained by heaven for unless man were like God and knew everything, it is better he should know nothing. If he knows one fact only, instead of profiting by it, it will land him in the soup. (B & W Publishing, 1922)

Buchan may be right, but this can be an interesting way of bringing conflict into a story of time-travel or time-slip. Other hazards that can be encountered by your characters are:

◆ disappointment with the past or future
◆ inability to cope with their unfamiliarity
◆ the danger of being marooned in another time
◆ possible damage to the present if anything is altered.

Whether this damage would occur or not has been explored by many writers. In Ray Bradbury's story *A Sound of Thunder* the accidental destruction of one insect by a time-traveller visiting the age of the dinosaurs changes the world of the present to which he returns. Other writers have the time-travellers perform the very actions that shape the present, with chilling results in Garry Kilworth's *Let's Go to Golgotha* and with gloriously funny results in Harry Harrison's *The Technicolour Time Machine*.

J.B. Priestley considered that it was legitimate to allow a man to visit the past as an observer but not to let him take action: if the time-traveller was to act in another time than his own, he suggested, the protagonist must occupy another body.

All these devices are staples of children's SF. Children like the chance to pit their wits vicariously against the conditions of other times.

Alternative worlds

Stories set in alternative worlds which have come about because at some crisis point in history a battle was lost instead of won, or an heir to a kingdom died causing a different dynasty to come to the throne is another popular sub-genre. Joan Aiken has written several books set in a world where the Stuarts are on the throne and the Hanoverians are pretenders. Diana Wynne Jones's 'Chrestomanci' books are set in a parallel world where witchcraft is the norm and ordinary mortals are deviants.

Golden rules for fantasy and SF writers

- ◆ The more unusual the scene, the more ordinary the main characters should be.
- ◆ In SF an important element of the story is a law or set of facts that are known by the reader to be untrue, but the amount of untrue facts should be small: you need change only one thing to alter reality and make it SF or fantasy.
- ◆ In creating a secondary world there must be familiar things as well as marvels otherwise the reader finds it hard to relate to it. There must be plenty of detail, and even if he is not going to use every item, the writer should know the history as well as the geography, the economy, the energy sources and what the people eat and how they dress. He must know how the planet or country is ruled and policed, whether it is warlike or peace-loving. An excellent site that lists questions you may need to answer world building is:

www.sfwa.org/writing/worldbuilding1.htm.

◆ Don't overlook the possibilities of SF stories for the 5–7 age group: they like stories of robots, spacemen and alien monsters.

◆ When you think of conflict, don't forget the possibilities of culture conflict – the visitors from earth versus the aliens, or the people from now versus the people of then.

◆ There must be a theme behind the story, a point to be made. Be sincere.

◆ Be optimistic about man's future: even when your story pinpoints a flaw, show it can be corrected.

◆ Don't underestimate children's curiosity about the future: warn them about things that bother you, show them your Utopia and enjoy using your imagination!

Animal stories

1. Animal families

Picture books and series books for 5–7s are often about humanised animals because:

◆ Little children find it easy to identify with animals.

◆ Animals do not carry connotations of class, race or colour: the writer chooses Daddy Bear, Mummy Bear and Baby Bear as his protagonists, making his story universally acceptable.

◆ An animal-child can do things that would be dangerous/naughty for a human child. George the monkey in H.E. Rey's *Curious George* does wonderfully naughty things that any child would love to do but dare not; and being a monkey, he gets away with them.

These books for young children are a mixture of the reality of domestic life and the fantasy of having animals talking and doing things human beings do.

2. Animals in a fantasy world

In fairy tale and fantasy, animals can talk to humans, they are sometimes magic and can do unusual things, but they will make more impact if they retain characteristics of the real animal. In the Narnia books animals in battle don't use swords, but hooves and teeth as animals would in nature. Sometimes animals don't speak but communicate by thought transference, particularly in science fiction stories.

3. Half real, half fantasy

This is the hybrid story with humans and animals in a natural situation but in which the animals talk to each other but are not heard or understood by humans. *Charlotte's Web* by E.B. White is an example of this popular genre.

4. The life stories of wild animals

They should be portrayed as they live, complete with their environment and their struggles with their natural enemies as in *Tarka the Otter* by Henry Williamson and *The Story of a Red Deer* by J.W. Fortescue.

There are problems in this kind of story. Skilled writing is called for, as is accurate knowledge of the animal and its environment, and a clear idea of the mores one is going to portray. For in order to bring the animal to life you have to supply him with human emotions, thoughts and speech – and we can only guess what is probable.

We know animals are good mothers so it is justifiable to use the maternal instinct in stories, but we also know that animals are unsentimental and will often sacrifice the weakest in a litter for the good of the strong ones. Should we share this aspect of their instinct with children who will probably feel this is grossly unfair and be upset? How do we deal with animal deaths without being sentimental and/or melo-dramatic? Wild animals force the writer and the reader to take sides, especially if the animals are carnivorous. One animal's triumphant finding of a meal is another animal's tragic death.

5. The life story of a domestic animal
The prototype is *Black Beauty* by Anna Sewell, which was written to plead for better treatment for horses. Since then many books have told the life story of a domestic animal, or of the taming of animals such as the otters in *Ring of Bright Water* by Gavin Maxwell.

Many people have a beloved cat or dog and think that a book about the life story of their pet would make a good children's book, but at the present time this is not a popular genre with publishers.

For younger children, the story of a child and his hamster, say, can be used to teach the best way to care for a pet, but there must be more to the story than didacticism – children love to learn, but they are suspicious of morals.

6. An animal as a minor character
Animals can be used to help the plot or to add to the hero's characterisation, particularly a pet belonging to a child character, such as the hero's dog, Jumble, in Richmal

Crompton's 'William' books, and Tim in Enid Blyton's Famous Five stories. Animals give children who feel themselves to be underdogs a feeling of power. As Francie in *Francie and the Boys* by Meredith Daneman says about her dog, 'she could boss him around when other people bossed her, and comfort him when she felt like crying.'

These animals don't talk, but human motives and thoughts may still be attributed to them by the writer. Animals should be strongly characterised and can be used to bring about plot twists and to add humour.

7. Riding books
Horses and ponies provide the characters and the plot here. Although these stories are written from the young rider's point of view, the horses should also be strongly portrayed to individualise them.

At one time these books were wildly popular with young, pony-mad girls for whom riding was the most important thing in their lives. They were equally popular with girls who wished they could ride, for whom these stories were wish-fulfilment in the same way that Cinderella romances were for their elder sisters. Some editors nowadays feel this type of book is élitist but riding is still popular with pre-teen and early teenage girls, so if you write a pony book, choose your publisher carefully.

Golden rules for writing about animals
◆ Look at animal stories that are currently popular – Dick King-Smith's books are excellent examples.

- Scour the catalogues to see what type of animal books publishers are taking.
- Humanisation is more successful if something is preserved of the creature's animal nature. Beatrix Potter knew this, which is why Peter Rabbit goes to Mr McGregor's garden to steal vegetables.
- Animals in alliance or juxtaposition should reflect nature. The Foxy Gentleman, for instance, is the natural enemy of Jemima Puddleduck; in Tom and Jerry cartoons, the natural pecking order of 'cat hates mouse, and dog hates cat' is adhered to. So if you decide to write a story about a pirate cat, it is better not to have mice for his crew, but rather have the pirate cat fighting a ship full of mice.
- Be true to the animals you write about. As Richard Adams author of *Watership Down* has said, animals should be allowed to keep their animalian dignity.
- Be sincere. Marjorie Fisher in *Intent Upon Reading* (Brockhampton Press, 1964), said, 'Silly books about animals are among the most corrupting influences children can meet.' Avoid the 'a-dear-little-pussy-cat-sat-on-the-mat' style that trivialises the animal and insults the reader.

Family stories

These are the slice-of-life stories that writers like Jacqueline Wilson do so well. In family stories characterisation is paramount. There must also be a problem of some kind that has to be worked through.

School stories

No longer the boarding school stories that were popular in the 30s and 40s. These are set in today's primary and comprehensive schools. Don't forget you will be writing for experts who know just what school is like, so be sure to get the details right.

Problem books

For the youngest readers the problems are simple: jealousy of a new baby, fear of the dark, worry over going to a new school or moving house. For pre-teens it can be dealing with unattainable longings such as owning a pony or dog, or wanting to be a princess or a pirate. This can be dealt with by using fantasy, or by showing your character coming to terms with something that is not possible. Older readers' problems can be dealing with bullies, newly awakened sexual feelings or coping with dysfunctional families.

The rattling good yarn

This is the adventure story of the Ransome or Blyton type, driven by the plot, but needing good characterisation. Many adventure themes have become hackneyed and new ones need to be devised. Instead of foiling crooks, try a green theme such as foiling developers who threaten a beautiful piece of countryside, or send your characters to the rescue of a hostage as in Peter Dickinson's *The Twelfth Raven* and K.M. Peyton's *Prove Yourself a Hero*.

Historical novels

Historical novels, which have been out of fashion for some years, have made a come back. Books that fit in with periods being studied in the National Curriculum are sought by publishers. There are several series of diary books covering such periods that show what it was like to be a child living at the time. It goes without saying that any historical novel needs to be well researched, and a new slant can make a world of difference.

Improbable reality

This is the real world with a magic ingredient. Diana Wynne Jones in *The Ogre Downstairs* deals with two families trying to adjust when the mother of one set of children marries the father of another. A magical chemistry set is the fantasy ingredient that causes adventures and finally unites them.

Anarchic children

This is Roald Dahl country; the setting is the real world but the child characters are outrageous as is his *Matilda*, Andrew Davies's *Marmalade Atkins* and Gene Kemp's Tyke in *The Turbulent Term of Tyke Tyler*. Children love to read about naughtiness.

Horror and ghost stories

Horror is obviously not for the very young, but it is popular with the pre-teens and teenagers. Ghost stories can be for all ages, but you need to use a light touch and inject humour in ghost stories for the very young.

EXERCISES

1. Make a list of the things that you think would appeal to children in the age group for which you intend to write. For instance, your list might read, *bicycles*, *secret codes*, *mysterious parcels*, *computers*. How would you use some of these in one of the above genres?

2. Make a list of your own special interests and see whether one of them could be used in a children's story. For instance, such apparently grown-up interests as patchwork and gardening have been successfully used.

3. Think about animals. How would you use them in your own stories?

3

Who is Going to Read your Book?

Don't ever start a story without a clear idea of the age group you are targeting. Different ages have different needs. The various genres discussed in the previous chapter must be carefully tailored for the different age groups.

PICTURE BOOKS – 0–6 YEAR OLDS

Many writers shy away from picture books because they cannot draw, but you can simply provide text and the publisher will choose an artist to illustrate your words.

Don't get a friend, (unless your friend is already known as a book illustrator) to do the pictures, it may spoil both your chances. Publishers are reluctant to take on an untried artist as well as an untried writer.

If you are a writer *and* an artist, then the pictures and the words will grow together. Don't do all the illustrations for the book before getting the publisher's approval, do two sample pictures (one in colour and one black and white) and a story-board with roughs. Always send photocopies of your samples. Original artwork is valuable and should not be sent until it is asked for.

How long should it be?

The length of text for a picture book is seldom less than 500 words or more than 2,000, but it is better to think in pages. Picture books are usually 32 pages, including the covers, end-papers and prelims (publishing information), so you should aim for 24 pages of text.

Write your story concisely, then cut and polish. Audrey Wood, who writes picture book texts says, 'I check my MS word by word, line by line, evaluating every sentence for excitement, visual impact, rhythm, variety and colourful word usage. Then I ask, What can be eliminated? What can be substituted?'

Write rhythmically, use repetitive phrases. Aim for simplicity and clarity. Read your story aloud to check for rhythm and flow. It must stand being read over and over again. If possible, try it out on children. If they fidget or seem bored, you know you have more work to do.

Write very visually. This helps the illustrator as well as the reader. As you write each caption think, 'Can this be illustrated?' Don't have sitting and thinking scenes without action. And remember, little children have a short attention span, so keep the story moving.

What shall I write about?

You need simple ideas for this age group. The whole world is so new to them that everything is intriguing. A successful picture book answered the simple question – 'What does

Mummy have in her handbag?'

When looking for ideas think 'what would make me happy if I were a child?' Remember the child's eye view is different from yours: get down on your hands and knees and see what the world looks like if your eye level is three feet above the ground.

- Stories about toys, animals or household objects are all suitable for this age group.
- Stories in which animals behave like humans with a Mummy, a Daddy and a child work well because very small children identify easily with the animal-child.
- Stories about families are popular especially those dealing with everyday problems like not wanting to go to bed.

Use emotion

'In a good picture book, whatever the surface image might be, there is an underlying emotional truth that relates to the lives of the children,' said an American picture-book editor. 'The thing that grabs them is if you involve their feelings.'

Joy and love must be fully realised; anxiety over the fate of a lost object gives tension, but the object must be found in the end. Always leave this age group feeling happy and safe.

Universal appeal

Picture books in full colour are expensive to produce so publishers like to get a publisher in another country on board so that the illustrations can be used with translated text. This means that subjects must have universal appeal. For instance, a picture book about Guy Fawkes and Bonfire Night is unlikely to succeed because it celebrates a purely British festival. Going to Grandma's house or going to the beach, however, is much more likely to be acceptable.

Golden rules for picture book writers

◆ The key words in writing picture book scripts are, **brevity**, **originality**, and **emotion**.

◆ The picture book market is hard to crack, so if your script is not successful, try again. Even experienced authors don't achieve success with every script: if one in every five is accepted, they are content.

◆ For a clearer understanding of picture book construction, look in your library for *The Art of Maurice Sendak* by Selma Lanes (Bodley Head, 1980).

BEGINNING READERS – 5–7 YEAR OLDS

Children who have just learned to read need simple stories to read by themselves. Most publishers have a series of books for this group, with different length requirements. See list (Figure 2), which is correct at time of going to press, but liable to change – so check publishers' new books, and write for author guidelines.

◆ Keep sentences and paragraphs short.

◆ Try for a light, breezy style. Read several books before you begin to write to absorb the mood and tone.

◆ Keep the action going and the characters moving. Even when they are speaking, characters should be doing something: a child's attention is halved as soon as characters are motionless.

◆ Make sure your characters behave like real children of

CHILDREN'S SERIES BOOKS

Series	Age	Wordage	Publisher
Leapfrog	3-5	5/700	Franklin Watts
Story Books	4-7	6/10,000	Walker Books
(Several stories around one character)			
Young Fiction	5-7	2,500	Bloomsbury
Corgi Pups	5-8	15/2,500	Transworld
Yellow Story Books	5-7	2,000	HarperCollins
My First Read Alone	5	1,500	Hodder Children's
I Am Reading	5-6	1,500/2,000	Kingfisher
Crunchies	5-7	1/1,500	Orchard
Young Puffins	5-6	1,500	Penguin Group
Blue Bananas	5-7	1/1,500	Egmont Children's
Rockets	5-7	1,200	A & C Black
(4 linked stories 1,200 each)			
Story Books	5-7	6,000	Egmont Children's
(4 linked stories around a character)			
Bright Stars	5-7	700	Hodder
Young Hippo	5-9	3,500/10,000	Scholastic
Shooting Stars	6-8	1,500/1,750	Hodder
Tigers	6-9	3/5,000	Andersen Press
Jets	6-9	2,000	A & C Black
Young Corgi	6-9	3/6,000	Transworld
Read Alone	6-7	2/4,000	Hodder Children's
Yellow Story Books	6-8	2,000	Hodder Children's
Colour Young Puffin	6-7	3,000	Penguin Group
Sprinters	6-8	2,000	Walker Books
Racers	7-10	7,500/15,000	'' ''
Middle Fiction	7-9	6,000	Bloomsbury
Red Story Books	7-9	6/8,000	HarperCollins
Colour Jets	7-10	2,000	'' ''
Story Book	7-9	8/12,000	Hodder Children's
Red Story Books	7-9	2,500	'' '' ''
Tremors	7-10	2,500	'' '' ''
Scientists	7-10	2,500	'' '' ''
History Story Books	7-10	2,500	'' '' ''
Yellow Bananas	7-9	3,000	Egmont
Chillers	8-10	4,500	A & C Black
Hippo	8-11	20/25,000	Scholastic
Corgi Yearling	8-11	16/20,000	Transworld
Corgi 10+	10+	20/30,000	Transworld
Bantam 10+	10+	25/45,000	Transworld
Red Apples	9-11	15/25,000	Orchard Books
Surfers	9-12	13,000	Penguin Group
Reads	9-11	15,000	Egmont

Fig. 2. List of publishers' series.

today, and that their dialogue reflects the way real children speak. Don't use old fashioned slang like *Golly*, *Gosh* and *Super*. Keep slang to a minimum.

◆ Use humour as much as possible. Children love jokes and want to laugh. Aim to make reading your story fun.

◆ Write visually and vividly.

What sort of story for these readers?

◆ Slice-of-life stories about situations they can recognise: beginning school, coping with siblings, family stories.

◆ Fantasy stories about witches and wizards, dragons and dinosaurs, giants and goblins, even ghosts if these aren't *too* scary. Remember, if you are planning gruesome scenes, children are less upset by something remote from their own life – say a pirate killed in his lair – than by a strange shadow in their own bedroom.

◆ If you make the ghost, the villian or dragon funny, then children will enjoy the scary frisson.

◆ Magic with unexpected results can make a hilarious story but it must be used with care. It must fit into the story and be prepared for, so that it seems reasonable and believable.

◆ Stories with animals in them. Children love to read about animals interacting with humans and playing a pivotal role in the story. Good examples are Colin West's *Monty* books in the Jets series.

SERIES BOOKS – 7–9 YEAR OLDS

As you will see from the list (Figure 2), this age group has series books too. These are longer than the beginning readers, but still written to strict lengths. Most of the rules given for the younger series books apply for this group, and similar types of stories but for these you can have a few more characters and more incidents.

TWEEN-AGERS – 9–12 YEAR OLDS

These are books that run from 15,000 words to 30,000 words and do not fit into a series, but stand alone. They can be in any of the genres listed in the previous chapter. The fact that it is not going to be part of a series gives you greater freedom in choosing your subject and your style. For instance, if you wanted to write your book as a collection of letters or the diary of your main character, this would not fit into a series, but could make an excellent stand-alone book.

There are some important points to bear in mind when writing for the children of today.

1. We are aiming for an equal opportunity society so:
   ◆ Use a good mix of boys and girls in your stories.
   ◆ Don't always make the leader of the gang a boy.
   ◆ Let the girls do daring things as well as the boys.
   ◆ Remember that mothers as well as fathers often go out to work these days.
2. We live in a multi-racial society so:
   ◆ Use a mix of black, white and brown people.
   ◆ Don't have just one child from an ethnic minority in a class; this doesn't reflect reality, especially in inner city schools.
3. We try to write with fairness about all sorts and conditions of people so:
   ◆ Neither you as the author, nor your characters, should

be patronising or condescending.
◆ Don't preach or moralise – you are writing a story, not
  a tract.

However, keep a sense of proportion. Don't go overboard
with political correctness, but bear in mind the points
mentioned.

TEEN FICTION – YOUNG ADULT BOOKS

After the age of 11 or 12 although many children begin reading
adult books, they still like to read about people in their teens,
and as YA books are shorter than adult novels – 20–40,000
words – readers often find them easier to cope with. Most
publishers of children's books have a list for this age group.

Recently this aspect of children's publishing has become more
important. For the first time ever a children's book was
awarded the Whitbread Prize in 2002. Philip Pullman's novel
for teenagers, the third book in the *His Dark Materials* trilogy,
The Amber Spyglass, (Scholastic 2000) was the winner. It
cannot be long before J.K. Rowling's Harry Potter books will
be aimed at 11+ readers as Harry ages a year in each book.

The rewards for children's writers are improving, too.
Macmillan bought Lady Georgia Byng's book *Molly Moon's
Incredible Book of Hypnotism,* for which she has been paid
£1 million.

Books for this age group should always have teenagers as the
main characters and should be told from a teenage point of
view. (More about Viewpoint in Chapter 6.)

Very few subjects are taboo here, as long as controversial issues are sensitively handled. You should neither minimise difficulties nor pile on the agony to be sensational and above all, you must be sincere. Character and theme are often more important than plot in YA books, emotion is important too.

Subjects for YA books

Besides the genres mentioned in the previous chapter, YA books can be about:

◆ *Fantasy*. This is far and away the most popular genre for YA books. Since the *Harry Potter* and *Lord of the Rings* films and the success of the *His Dark Materials* trilogy, there has been a surge of interest in this genre. Quest stories, alternate worlds, allegory, sword and sorcery, myths and legends are all used in the battle between good and evil which is the ultimate theme of most fantasies.

◆ *The supernatural*. Stories about witches, vampires, ghosts and other aspects of the supernatural are popular with this age group.

◆ *The future*. Stories set in our world in the future, as well as science fiction stories set in space and on other worlds go down well.

◆ *Romance*. Light-hearted love stories, serious ones about awakening sexuality, romance and mystery, romance and comedy are all popular fare.

◆ *Friendship*. Either the togetherness of friends or their growing apart for some reason.

◆ *Rite of passage*. Finding one's identity or the moment of becoming an adult is often explored in YA books.

◆ *Thrillers and mysteries* solved by teenage sleuths, both light-hearted and serious are good for this group.

- *Horror stories*. These can be really strong as the readers are probably already reading James Herbert and Stephen King. This is the age group at whom horror movies are aimed.
- *Survival books*. These can be about surviving battles with the elements, surviving poverty, plague, anorexia, pregnancy, being gay – even surviving the difficulties of everyday family life.
- *Sports books*. Stories about soccer are popular with boys; snooker has featured in a recent teenage book. There is room for books using other sports as background material.
- *Historical stories and time slip*. These have had a lean time recently, but they are now popular, especially Ancient History.
- *Humour*. Light-hearted stories with plenty of laughs go down well with this age group.
- *Career books*. At one time this was staple fare for YA, but there haven't been many lately. Perhaps it is time for a new look at this neglected genre?

For young adults, it is not obligatory to have a happy ending: sorrow can be cathartic. But if you can, you should be upbeat and end on a note of hope.

Some imprints for young adult fiction

Collins – *Flamingo* for 14+
Hodder – *Bite*
Little Brown – *Orbit*
Random House Children's Books – *Definitions* 11+
Collins – *Voyager*, YA fantasy
Orchard Books – *Black Apples* 11+
Scholastic – *Point* 12+

Macmillan – *Young Picador* 12–15

EXERCISES

1. Find a suitable subject for a picture book and decide how you would tackle it.

2. Check out some series books and see how each imprint has its own style.

3. Take your favourite fairy tale from the Brothers Grimm and see how it could be modernised.

4. Get hold of a teen magazine and read the problem page and see if you can find the germ of a YA story there.

$$4$$

Plotting and Planning

'Where do you get your ideas? How do you find your plots?' are questions frequently asked of authors. Some people imagine there is a little-known shop called *Plots 'R' Us*, but the answer is, if you are alert and have your mind open, there are story ideas all around you waiting to be used.

The most basic plot of all which can be used in any number of ways is:

1. Somebody wants something.
2. They can't have it.
3. They strive to get it.
4. They either get it or learn to do without it.

HOW TO FIND PLOT IDEAS

◆ Read your daily newspaper looking for news items that suggest stories. (See Figure 3, for example.)
◆ Start with a concept, an idea that encapsulates a story in a sentence. *Alice in Wonderland* reduced to its concept is: A girl falls down a rabbit hole and finds herself in a strange world.
◆ An overheard snatch of conversation can hold the germ of a story. 'If you think I'm going to do what *she* says, you're

dafter that I thought!' or 'Marion never liked James because of his ears.'

♦ A line from a song can suggest a plot. For instance, *'Everyone's Gone to the Moon* might be the germ of a science fiction story.

Fig. 3. Collage of newspaper cuttings.

♦ People you notice, or faces in pictures, can start you off on a story. (More on this in Chapter 5.) If you start with people, make sure two of them are opposed to one another to give you conflict. If you choose one main character, give him a problem to solve.

♦ What do children want that they can't have? Think of a story that gives it to them. Children love the idea of wish fulfilment.

- If you read a story and are dissatisfied with the way it turns out, use this as a starting point. Write a new second half, change the names and the setting.

- Use a well-known book as a framework for your story. Books as different as *Bridget Jones's Diary* by Helen Fielding and *Lions and Liquorice* by Kate Fenton use the bones of Jane Austen's *Pride and Prejudice* as their bases.

- A place can be a starting point. A visit to a stately home might set you thinking about its past, or an unusual house might intrigue you. A churchyard glimpsed at night might give you creepy thoughts and inspire a ghost story.

- Looking at ordinary things from an unusual angle can be useful. Suppose every thousandth bicycle made had magic powers ... Any inanimate object endowed with supernatural powers can trigger a story.

- Small advertisements in local papers can offer intriguing possibilities, especially if you happen to misread words. (I once misread an advertisement for a Simmental bull as a sentimental bull.)

- You can build your plot from an emotion such as *jealousy*. You could explore this through a young child's feelings about the arrival of a new baby, or those of the second child in a family who is jealous of his older brother's success on the football field, or it could be a poor child jealous of a richer one. You could get a dozen different stories from that one emotion alone.

- Themes can be your starting point: sayings like, 'Be careful what you wish for, you may get it,' or 'Every action has a consequence.' Fantasy or reality can be used to illustrate such themes.

- Lost and found. (This is a variation on the basic plot we began with.) You could write a simple picture book about a mislaid teddy bear or someone's best green socks. Lost and found can be the basis of a fantasy about a lost jewel or talisman, the quest to find it can become a picaresque journey complete with villains, enchanters, monsters and hazards that will fill a book for 8–12 year olds.

◆ Answer the child's question – 'Where do lost things go?' as in Mary Norton's *The Borrowers* and Hans Andersen's *Tin Soldier*.

◆ Brainstorming charts can be fruitful. Put a word in the centre of a page, and round it write others suggested by the central word, then new words suggested by the secondary words. This can give you a plot idea. (See Figure 4 for an example of a brainstorming chart.)

◆ Use fairy or folk tales with imagination.

   1. The picaresque tale or journey is the basis of *Puss in Boots*, *Don Quixote*, *Pickwick Papers*, and *Tom Jones*.

   2. Reversal of fortune is the basis of *The Ugly Duckling*, *Cinderella*, *Ivanhoe*, *The Little Princess*, and *The Mayor of Casterbridge*.

   3. Victory against overwhelming odds is the basis of *Jack and the Beanstalk*, *David and Goliath*, *Rumpelstiltskin*, and *Huntingtower*.

   4. Lover with nothing to recommend him is the basis of *Beauty and the Beast*, *The Frog Prince* and any number of women's romances and can be used in teenage fiction.

   5. Use a prophecy and arrange that the steps taken to avoid it actually bring it about, as in *Sleeping Beauty* and *Oedipus*.

   6. Invert the sex of main character so that Tom the piper's son becomes Thomasina the piper's daughter.

   7. Invert the relative ages of the characters so that Cinderella is older than the Ugly Sisters.

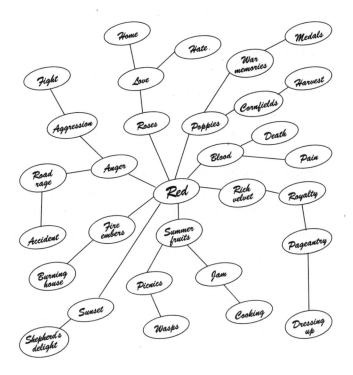

Fig. 4. 'Brainstorming' chart.

◆ Take a story and change the period – imagine an historical incident set in the present, or something happening now set in the past.

KEEPING TRACK OF YOUR IDEAS

In Chapter 1, the importance of keeping a notebook in which to jot down story ideas as they occur was stressed. As your notebooks become filled with concepts, titles of books you want to read, quotations, facts about something that interests you, and bits of description, it is a good idea to separate the story concepts so they are easily accessible.

Using a card index

Copy the ideas onto 3″ × 5″ index cards and put them in a box divided into categories that suit your kind of writing: Picture books, Fantasy, Science Fiction, Supernatural, Historical, Romance, or any other category that appeals to you.

When a day comes that you can't decide what to write next, get out your concept cards and lay them out as if playing patience. Keep shuffling, laying out and discarding until one idea strikes and sparks off another, then go on to develop a plot. (See Figure 5 for an example of index cards with plot ideas.)

Using a spike

Some writers cannot be persuaded to use notebooks, but scribble notes on old envelopes, the backs of shopping lists or paper napkins. If this is your style, buy an old-fashioned bill spike and spike your notes. Then at least you have them all in one place when you are searching for a vital piece of information.

Making a master index

Number the pages of your notebooks, and also number your notebooks. (I am currently on notebook no. 34.) Buy an indexed book (like an address book) and put in headings for your interests. For instance, under W, among other things, I have – Witches, Weddings, Wills, Wool, Wigs, Writer's block. When a notebook is full, go through and if you have a note on witches on page 14 of notebook no. 28, in your index book write: 28/14. This saves time when you are hunting

At the fair there was something strange
about two of the horses on the merry-go-round.
A child finds that riding on one he goes into
the future and on another he goes back into the
past. Describe the terrible sense of loss and
deprivation when the fair moves on and he no
longer can take these adventures. Sort of 'I
ceased to be a child the day the circus left
town'.

A story about childhood of a witch.
Bk 20/25 This becomes Lory + the
DRAGON

She was a child who expected
the wonderful as a matter of course.
She imagined she was a princess
who had been stolen in turn [stolen]
and/or peril and then lost/abandoned
by those who stole her

Fig. 5. Sample index cards.

around for a note you made two years ago. See Figure 6 for
sample page of index book.

HOW DO YOU DEVELOP YOUR IDEAS?

You use Rudyard Kipling's six honest serving men –

'Their names are What and Why and When
And How and Where and Who.'

Take your plot idea and decide:

- ◆ *What* is the story about? *What* happens next? *What* is also useful as in 'what if this were to happen?'
- ◆ *Why* can't your hero achieve his goal right away? Think of obstacles and challenges you can put in his way.
- ◆ *When* is all this happening? Is it past, present or future? Work out a time sequence, especially if something has to be achieved by a certain time, a plus which gives a book pace.
- ◆ *How* do your characters do what they have to do? *How* also covers any research that needs to be done.
- ◆ *Where* does the story take place? Decide on the setting.
- ◆ *Who* are the characters? *Who* will play out this drama? See Chapter 5 for characterisation.

THE THREE PARTS OF A PLOT

A story begins with a situation (the status quo): something happens to disturb it; the disturbance is the story and it ends when a different status quo is established.

1. Hooking the reader (the beginning)

It is vital that you have an exciting beginning. Begin at, or just before, a moment of change that is going to bring about the disturbance. (More about how to handle beginnings in Chapter 6.)

2. Holding the reader (the middle)

The two Cs are paramount here – Conflict and Complications. Conflict doesn't have to be a row or fight, anything that upsets the smooth running of life counts as conflict in a story.

SEWING	3/11 - 3/27 - 4/74 - 15/50 19/110
SHOPPING	3/41-44 -
STONES (Standing)	8/30 - 9/33ff
STEPMOTHERS	9/30-33
SPELLS	10/22
SMUGGLERS	17/116 - 3/84 - 22/42ff - 25/6
SWORDS	5/64 - 6/31 - 8/45
SPYING	4/92 - 5/23

Fig. 6. Page from index book.

Major conflicts
- male against male, male against female, female against female
- protagonist against group
- group against group
- person or group against nature or the elements
- animal(s) against nature or mankind
- child or children against adults
- conflict of decision: which of two courses should protagonist take?
- puzzle to be solved.

Minor conflicts
- failure
- opposition
- deflation
- death
- denial
- surprise
- argument
- disapproval
- disillusion
- discovery
- problem
- mystery
- resistance
- mistake
- new character(s) introduced into a group
- mechanical device going wrong
- bad weather
- serious illness.

Creating complications

Don't make things too easy. The scales must be weighted against your hero or heroine, their task must be as difficult as possible. Each time you get your main character out of difficulty, get him into another conflict. This way you build up incidents and show character. A creative writing tutor once advised, 'Get your character up a tree; throw stones at him. Get him down, but let him drop straight into a cooking pot. Light a fire under him and as the water gets too hot to bear, get him out.' In other words, make as much trouble for him as you can.

Your object is to arouse the maximum of suspense, apprehension and expectancy in your reader. Just as he sighs with relief at the hero's deliverance, another difficulty must come along. Don't make the mistake of the old comic-book writers who used the device, 'With one bound he was free!' Let your solution to a dilemma come from the hero's cleverness or from a noble trait in his character or from a plausible outside influence.

Another way to heighten tension is to put into your story something forbidden (as happens in many fairy tales) that, if the taboo is broken, will result in dire consequences. Then you make one of the characters do the forbidden thing:

◆ from necessity
◆ forgetting it was forbidden
◆ from bravado.

This ploy involves readers closely with the story, making them want to shout 'look-out-behind-you' and warn the character. It also produces other incidents and further trials for your characters.

3. Payoff time – the end

Plan a satisfactory climax with all the loose ends tied up. Crises can be greatly improved by turning the moment of drama into a black moment when all seems lost and your characters are in despair. This will have your readers on the edge of their seats wondering – Will they, won't they survive/win through? (More about endings in Chapter 8.)

WHAT NOT TO WRITE

There are some cliché stories that editors have seen over and over again that are best avoided unless you can think of a brilliant new way to use them.

Most people would have said boarding school stories were completely outdated until J.K. Rowling came along with a startling original version, sending Harry Potter to Hogwarts School of Witchcraft and Wizardry. What child could resist the lure of a school where meals are feasts, pupils sleep in four-poster beds, the lessons are about magic and the treatment for shock is eating blocks of chocolate?

Caroline Sheldon, authors' agent, says Sammy the Squirrel, Cyril the Slug and Teddy the Traffic Light are yesterday's rejects. These types of 'twee' characters have had their day. Whatever you do, don't be cosy, cute or coy.

Editors see with monotonous regularity stories about Father Christmas being helped by children to deliver presents, but occasionally a really outstanding one such as Raymond Briggs's *Father Christmas* makes the grade.

Children saving the family fortunes by finding hidden treasure; being cut off by the tide; stumbling on secret panels and hidden rooms; children foiling thieves. All these were once fresh, exciting ideas but have become overused, cliché situations. If you want to use them, find a new way of doing so.

TESTING THE PLOT

When you have finally worked out your plot, test by asking:

- Is there a beginning, a middle and an end?
- Are there believable characters?
- Is there plenty of conflict?
- Is there a problem to be solved?
- Is the ending satisfying?

If the answer is *yes*, go ahead: if not, think again.

Do I need an outline?

There is no rule that says you must have an outline but most writers find one useful. Much depends on the length of the story. If you are writing a younger children's story of 500–2,000 words, you probably don't: your concept with one or two incidents of conflict is enough. But if you are writing a book which may run to 35,000 words or more, an outline is useful: you will need a succession of scenes and obstacles to be overcome.

What is an outline?

An outline is a list of the scenes in your story. A scene is a unit of action and the reaction to it. Think in scenes, not in chapters, you will find it easier. Here are two methods of preparing an outline:

1. Think on paper

Tell yourself the bare bones of the story, keep asking yourself questions about it and write down the answers. For example '. . . and then she goes into the cave but she can't get out.' Why can't she? The tide has come in and she forgot to bring a rope. No, that's a cliché situation – think of something else. Perhaps she ties a message to the dog's collar . . . Who will rescue her? and so on.

Don't go into too much detail at this stage otherwise you won't have any fun writing the book. Half the pleasure of writing is surprising yourself in small ways as you go along. You are not bound to follow your outline, you may think of a better idea than your first one, or your characters become so real they dictate to you. You may find yourself saying, 'I didn't know she was going to do/say that!'

2. Put each scene onto a card

6″ × 4″ index cards, or separate pages of a loose-leaf book are best for this, giving you space to put in snatches of dialogue as they occur to you, and to add further developments. The cards or pages can be moved about to change the order of the scenes and new ones can be slotted in as new ideas occur.

I don't like the idea of planning

If this is your sentiment, you are not alone. Many authors like to plunge in as soon as they have an idea and write to see what happens. There is no *right* way to write a book, each writer finds his own way. As Kipling said:

> There are nine and sixty ways
> Of constructing tribal lays
> And every single one of them is right.

Do I need a theme?

The theme of a book is usually an abstract idea like *friendship, loyalty, the quest for identity,* or *the fight between good and evil.* If you have an underlying theme and make every scene point it up, it strengthens the book. You do not state the theme in so many words, that would be as bad as pointing a moral; but the theme should be a subtle sub-text to your writing.

EXERCISES

1. Find a plot idea from a news item.

2. Read some fairy tales and see which could be the basis of a modern children's story.

3. Think back to your childhood: what did you want that you never got? Could you use this as the basis of a story?

4. Take a concept from your notebook and apply Kipling's Serving Men to it.

5

Characters and How to Find Them

Characterisation is the most important element in the making of memorable fiction. The world's most exciting plot if it features cardboard characters will be as unappetising as yesterday's rice pudding. At the centre of every good story there should be someone involved in a situation so fundamental that almost any reader can identify with him.

WHICH COMES FIRST, CHARACTER OR PLOT?

It's a bit like asking, which came first, the chicken or the egg?

Sometimes a writer has a great idea for a story and needs characters to make it work. In this case, the characters are servants of the idea, so he decides their *function* in the story and creates people who can do what is required. To visualise the character, it can help to think of an actor you would cast if your story were being filmed.

Sometimes the writer creates a character about whom he wants to write a story. In this case, the nature of the character will suggest a plot. Diana Wynne Jones says she often has characters growing in her mind who are looking for stories.

Do you take your characters from life?

All writers plunder their own lives and those of their friends and acquaintances for material, but it seldom works to take a complete person from life. True, you can see their looks, but you cannot know how their minds work; also if they recognise themselves you may offend them. You can take part of person A, (say, her mannerisms and her hair) and combine it with the face and body of person B, but her thoughts and ideas must come from your imagination.

Another way of finding characters is to make a collection of pictures taken from magazines. Always be on the lookout for faces that interest you. When you are planning your stories, go through your picture file.

How many characters do you need?

The answer is the smallest number necessary to make your plot work. One of the biggest pitfalls for the children's writer is having too many characters.

Which characters must you have?

Characters can be divided into five groups:

1. The principals

A hero and/or heroine (protagonists) and a villain (antagonist) must be there. These are the essential characters and they should develop and grow during the story. These are the ones whose background details you need to know.

Antagonists are not necessarily wicked, but you need someone who can/will frustrate the main character's achievement or goal. You need conflict between characters to keep up tension.

Children like the main character to be someone their own age or a little older. They like to imagine themselves as the hero. But they can also identify with other characters:

◆ Someone with characteristics they recognise as being childlike such as a young man entering adulthood. Rosemary Sutcliff used this type of hero frequently in books like *The Eagle of the Ninth*.

◆ Someone who rebels against authority for a good reason such as Spiderman or Robin Hood.

◆ Animals who are in conflict with humans; think *Peter Rabbit* or *Tarka the Otter*.

◆ Younger sons/daughters, outlaws, handicapped people and underdogs, as frequently found in fairy tales. Children often feel helpless because they are subject to what they consider the whims of adults. Even when the reasons are explained to them, they are often too self-centred to be won over. For this reason, children are frequently at odds with adults.

Arthur Ransome said, 'Stresses and strains have to be set up between the heroes and other children or grown-ups.'

Robert Westall said books for children had to be 'about the struggle between children and adults. It is this that interests children.'

2. Secondary characters

These are people within the main characters' circle who are there as sounding boards and as contrast to the main characters. They are less complex than the principals. Choose a few descriptive words to characterise them and don't go much beyond that. Example: Hilda – blonde plaits; helpful and loyal. Paul – tall and gangly; clumsy and jokey.

3. Background characters

Their function is to give reality and texture to the story. They are of varying importance. Most can be sketched in lightly unless they have a vital part to play. For instance, in a school-based story, they are the others in our hero's class; parents, teachers, friends of his parents. They are like the extras in a movie.

4. Wild cards

These are not essential characters, but can give added texture. They are over-the-top characters, often comic, larger than life. They don't grow and change. They are there as foils to the main characters. Mr. Micawber to David Copperfield, Gandalf to Bilbo Baggins, for instance. They often embody one main characteristic, such as greed, envy or generosity.

5. Walk-on parts

The waitress in a cafe, or the ticket collector whose function might be to make a single remark that sets the hero thinking. These need not even be named. They *are* their function or occupation: this is where you can use stereotypes.

NAMING YOUR CHARACTERS

It is said that some people look like their dogs, some people look like their cars, but everybody looks like his name. Therefore it is important to choose appropriate names, because names give out signals to the reader. People whose names actually signify character, such as Lady Sneerwell and Lord Foppington were used in the 18th century; Kingsley's Mrs.

Do-as-you-would-be-done-by and Scott's Laird of Killancureit were 19th century creations. Except for farce or allegory, this convention is seldom used today, but it is still useful to use strong names for strong characters and weak ones for weak characters. You don't expect Neville Longbottom to be as brave and clever as Harry Potter, but you do expect Draco Malfoy to be devious as soon as you see his name.

There are fashions in Christian names – they can be age and/or class indicators: use *The Guinness Book of Names* by Leslie Dunkling to help. This gives tables of the most popular Christian names for each year from 1900 to the present day.

Don't have several names starting with the same letter. Lucy and Louise in the same story can be confusing. Vary length and/or number of syllables.

Surnames can reveal ethnicity. Three-syllabled names sound grander than single syllables, double-barrelled names even grander. When in doubt, use place names taken from a gazetteer as surnames.

FAMILIES

It is important to build in friction points when you are creating a family. Besides the obvious conflict of the generation gap, your main character's place in the family can make a difference. The following are generalisations, but if you use them you will not go far wrong.

◆ *Only children* tend to be self-sufficient because they are on their own a lot. They fit in easily with adults because they spend more time with them than with their peers. An only girl child is often treated by her father as the son he didn't have, so she will follow boyish pursuits and will have confidence because her father concentrates on her and treats her as a worthwhile person.

◆ *Eldest children* are usually leaders and are prepared to take responsibility.

◆ *Second children* are fiercely competitive, vying with their older brother or sister.

◆ *Third* (and other middle children) are usually contrary: they have neither the assurance of the older ones nor the privileges of the babies. They have to be different to attract attention. These are the children whose constant cry is – 'It's not fair!'

◆ *The youngest* will be petted and spoiled, bullied and badgered in turn.

◆ *Twins* – writers tend to love them, editors tend to hate them! Only use twins if their twinship is essential to the plot. Don't be lazy and think one character dossier will do for both: twins have important differences of character. However, J.K. Rowling breaks this rule with Fred and George Weasley who are virtually interchangeable.

GETTING TO KNOW YOUR CHARACTERS

Besides using the checklist (see Figure 7), you can get to know characters better by pretending to be them. Write an account of your hero's life or background in his own voice. Or you can write a question and answer interview with him. For example:

Q. How many in your family, John?

<u>Character checklist</u>

Name: Age:

Birthdate: Birthplace:

Height: Weight:

Colour of hair: Colour of eyes:

Scars or Handicaps: Mannerisms/Habits:

Way of speaking:

Parents: Father's job:

Mother's job (if any):   Family's social status:

Relationship with parents: is father or mother preferred?

Brothers & Sisters: Place in family:

Kind of home: Education:

Attitude to life: Ambitions:

Friends, male or female friends preferred?

Best friend:

Any enemies or rivals?   Reasons for enmity:

Weakness or besetting sin:

Skills and interests:

Kinds of books & music preferred:

Favourite colours: Favourite foods:

Current problem and/or motivation:

What is this character afraid of?

What will make reader like/dislike this character?

What will make reader <u>remember</u> this character?

Fig. 7. Character checklist.

A. The grown-ups are Mum, Dad and Gran. My earwig of a brother is Mike – he's a year older than me, and doesn't he crow about it! There's my sister Rosie, she's five and gets in the way a lot, always asking questions. I don't let her into my room in case she tears my football posters; she would, you know, just for spite.

It is important to hear your character's voice in your head and both these exercises help with this. You never really know a character until you hear him speak.

Find your character inside yourself the way actors do when they are studying a part. When you have created the character and named him, you must *be* him: see through his eyes, feel what he feels, think his unique thoughts. Charles Dickens used to act out his characters in front of a mirror, thereby convincing one of his daughters that he was mad!

Beware of stereotypes – write against the grain. For instance, if you have a professor, don't make him absent-minded – that's a cliché! Make the absent-minded character the hero's father instead. There are clichés in looks too. If I had a pound for every green-eyed red-headed heroine I've seen in romantic MSS I would be very rich. Don't choose the first answer that comes to mind when planning: second thoughts are more interesting.

Differentiate characters of same age, sex and background. Especially with children in the same class at school, it is important to give them differences of looks, personality, and ways of speaking so that they are not interchangeable. Look, for example, at the three friends in Kipling's *Stalky & Co.*

PUTTING THE CHARACTERS ON THE PAGE
There are several ways of showing character:

1. *Description*: certain features are described
2. *Dialogue*: character is given a particular way of speaking
3. *Interaction*: how the character behaves with other people is shown
4. *Action*: what the character does
5. *Interior monologue*: the reader overhears what the character is thinking.

Description

Don't describe your characters in large chunks, but in small snippets spread through the narrative. Be impressionistic rather than exhaustive; show one or two salient features at a time. In the case of a minor character, one feature or mannerism may serve to flesh him out – a long nose, or bright blue eyes and freckles, or the way he always pulls his ear when thinking. When you give a character a tag of this sort, use it frequently.

Saying what a character is wearing can tell readers a lot about him or her. Compare:

> She wore a neat red dress and her shoes gleamed with fresh polish. Her dark hair had been brushed until it shone.

With:

> Her jeans were scruffy and her fawn shirt was torn. Mud encrusted her trainers, and it looked as if her tousled hair hadn't seen a comb that day.

Interaction

The villain barges into an old lady and knocks her shopping

flying and runs on. The hero stops and helps her up, dusts her down and picks her things up. You don't need to say one is callous and the other kind, you have shown it.

Action

Begin the story by showing the main character in action wherever possible. The reader begins to identify with the first character he meets in a book. If you don't bring in the hero at once, make the reader aware of him by making the opening conversation *about* him.

Reaction

Show your character's looks and personality by the reaction of others. In a famous comedy sketch two women are gossiping about a third.

> The first one says, 'You should see her kitchen!' The second says, 'I know. That woman's a stranger to Ajax.'

This tells more about the woman than a half page of description.

Dialogue

This has four purposes:

1. To show character.
2. To further action of plot.
3. To show the emotional state of the speaker.
4. To convey information. But beware: you must never let a character tell someone something he already knows just to inform the reader. So don't let a character say to his brother, 'Auntie Flo, our mother's sister who is married to

Uncle Albert and lives in Brighton, is coming to stay.'

Each person in your story should have a particular way of speaking. Some will use slang, others use long words. Some will use short sentences, some long ones. You can use speech tags as well as descriptive tags to indicate which character is speaking. Arthur Ransome's Nancy Blackett was always saying, 'Jibooms and bobstays!' and because of this, Ransome never had to add, 'Nancy said.'

Dialogue is important because you learn more about a person by what he says than the way he looks. (More about dialogue in Chapter 7.)

How do you make your readers like the hero/heroine?

◆ You make him do things the reader would love to do but can't.

◆ Show thoughts and actions with which readers will sympathise.

◆ Make him upright, honest, dependable, brave and clever but modest about it; but not all these characteristics at once.

◆ You make him the kind of person the reader would like to be, someone he envies.

◆ Don't make him a goody-goody – a few faults make a person more human (none of us is perfect). But let the faults be endearing. For instance, if you make him unreliable, let it be about time or remembering things, not about something important like keeping promises.

◆ Give him a sense of humour.

◆ Once he is established, make life difficult for him: if the odds are against him, the reader will be on his side.

- Focus on him: let other characters like him and say so to each other.
- Let the story be told from his point of view.

How do you make the reader dislike the villain?

- Make him do something loathsome or reprehensible. Being unkind to an animal will set most young readers against a character.
- Make him unreliable or untrustworthy. Let him be caught out telling lies.
- Make him speak harshly to a character you have made the reader like.
- Make him humourless.
- Make him a hypocrite.
- Let characters talk about his faults behind his back.
- Make him a smug smart-alec; nobody loves a know-it-all.

How do you make your main characters believable?

- You give them attitudes and reactions to what is happening and let the reader know either in dialogue or by overhearing their thoughts in interior monologue.
- You refer to their motive for doing things.
- You show them in scenes rather than telling about them in narration.
- You tell the story from their point of view.

Golden rules for character creation

- You must make your major characters interesting enough to hold your readers' attention. It is better to over-write the central characters than to under-write them.
- *You* must care about them otherwise no-one else will, but don't treat them with favouritism, giving them too smooth

a ride. They mustn't achieve their goal too easily.

- ◆ Because of their adventures, or what they have learned, your main characters must grow or change by the end of the story.
- ◆ Your minor characters must move the plot along or twist it or convey information, otherwise they are so much padding and should be cut.

EXERCISES

1. Plan a family group suitable for a story for 7–11 year olds, remembering to build in friction points.

2. Draw up a character dossier for a girl who is going to be the main character in a story for the 11+ age group.

3. Write out a question-and-answer interview with this girl.

4. You have an idea for a story (suitable for 9 year olds) about a boy who is terrified of going to a new school. Draw up a list of the people you will need for this story stating their functions, and make a dossier for the main character using the checklist.

5. Write a piece of dialogue that shows this boy's character and fears without him actually saying in so many words, 'I'm afraid of going to this new school.'

6

Beginnings

Having read so far, you have learned to think like a writer, you have chosen the age group for whom you are going to write and decided on the kind of story you are going to tackle. You have learned to expand an initial idea into a plot and to turn that into an outline. You have chosen your characters.

You are ready to begin writing your story.

HOW TO WRITE YOUR BOOK

The way to write a book is to write one sentence and then another and keep on doing it every day, rain or shine, sick or well. Just put something on paper: it won't be exactly what you want to say, no writer ever writes a thing decently the first time . . . Write something then keep on changing it until you are satisfied. You can be mighty sure of one thing, if you don't write anything, you won't have anything to change.

So wrote Kenneth Roberts in *Oliver Wiswell* (Collins, 1943).

Perseverence is vital. Professional writers write every day.

Some write for a certain number of hours, others aim at a quota of words for the day. If you have a full-time job or are running a home, try to set aside a particular writing time and make it regular. The longer you leave between writing sessions, the more likely you are to lose the mood or the thread of the story.

DEVELOPING STYLE

You already have several styles of your own. You use your personal style when you write a chatty letter to a friend, you use a formal style when you write a business letter and another style – probably a sort of shorthand – when you write in your notebook.

For writing a children's book you will develop another style suited to your subject matter:

- ◆ Keep your language simple.
- ◆ Avoid long sentences with subordinate clauses. Make the clause a new sentence without the conjuction.
- ◆ Avoid clichés and words of the moment.
- ◆ Think clearly.
- ◆ Write visually.
- ◆ Write to *express* not to *impress*.
- ◆ Keep descriptions short otherwise children will skip. Use your senses; what can your viewpoint character *see*, *hear*, *smell*, *feel (emotion)*, *touch (textures)?* What is the weather like?
- ◆ Children like colourful detail, so be specific. Frances Hodgson Burnett said, 'It is not enough to say they had tea, you must specify the muffins.'

Good grammar and good spelling are important. Use a dictionary to check, and a thesaurus for variety of vocabulary. If you are not sure about a point of grammar, look it up. *Write Right* by Jan Venolia is a good, small grammar book: Fowler's *Modern English Usage* is comprehensive.

POINT OF VIEW

You must decide from whose point of view you are going to tell the story. There are several to choose from.

First person

This is the 'I' book, the imaginary autobiography of the main character, which beginners often think is easiest. However, there are problems. If the narrator is a thirteen-year-old, you have to think yourself into his mind and use the vocabulary and sentence construction he would use if he were speaking. This can be difficult to sustain at book length, but if you can do it, it can be striking. Another disadvantage is that the narrator must be in every scene, or else be told what happens when he is off-stage, which can be awkward. Finally, children are said to dislike this type of story although I have never found it to be so. The advantage of using a first-person narrator is that the reader can easily identify with the key character.

Third person, single viewpoint

This is the usual viewpoint for children's books: everything is seen or commented on by the main character. Thus, *not* 'It was a sunny day which made the children feel good.' *but* 'The sunny day made Susan feel happy and she noticed it was having the same effect on the others.' This viewpoint also personalises the story, making the reader feel involved.

Omniscient author

This is the story in which the writer, like God, sees everything impartially. The author can see into the minds of all the characters and tell the reader what they are thinking as well as what they are doing. *Watchpoint*: don't as the Victorians did, address the reader over the characters' heads – 'It was this, dear reader, that was to be his downfall.' The advantage of the omniscient viewpoint is that the reader sees everything, but the disadvantage is that it is harder to get close to the main character.

Third person, multiple viewpoint

Most adult stories use this viewpoint. The reader is shown the action from the point of view of several different characters in turn, as if they are like the sisters in Greek myth who had only one eye which they shared, handing it from one to the other. The story is seen from the viewpoint of the character holding the eye. This means you can build up suspense with alternating narratives as in the old chestnut, 'Paul was now a prisoner. Meanwhile, back at the ranch . . .'

HOOKING THE READER

You must grab your reader on the first page, preferably in the first paragraph. An adult will allow you a page or two to get them into the story, but children decide whether to read a book or not much more quickly, therefore you must make your mark on the first page in a children's book.

You should provide action or *potential* action, or the mention of potential danger or upset. If there is little action, provide *promise* of action. These are the hooks that make your reader keep turning the pages.

Begin at a moment of change or crisis in the key character's life. Don't start with an explanation of his circumstances, or a description of where he lives. If you feel you need scene-setting and character establishment to get you going, write it for yourself and go on until you reach an action point. This is where your story should start:

- ◆ Start where the trouble begins.
- ◆ Start on the day that is different.
- ◆ Start where the main character comes up against something he can't stand.

Don't discard the previous material but feed it into the narrative in snippets as the story unfolds.

Some useful beginnings
Time words
The traditional time words with which to begin children's stories are 'Once upon a time' and 'Long, long ago'. Time words give a sense of movement and often imply future action which intrigues the reader. Words like *when*, *afterwards*, *sometimes*, and specific times like *every Thursday*, or *at dawn*.

When Rosie, who was only eight anyway, beat him doing ten lengths of the pool, it was the last straw.

from *Ordinary Jack* by Helen Cresswell
(Faber & Faber, 1977).

◆ This is where Jack finds something he can't stand.

One night Emma dreamt that she could fly **again**. It was a slight, dark, strange dream and she did not feel the effort of flying, the tight, difficult control of arms and legs that she had learned **two summers back**.

from *Emma in Winter* by Penelope Farmer (Chatto & Windus, 1966).

Three time words here that promise future action.

◆ This is the day that was different.

Opening with dialogue
Beginning a story with conversation is another attention grabber.

'Where is Papa going with that axe?' said Fern to her mother as they were setting the table for breakfast.

'Out to the hoghouse,' said Mrs Arable. 'Some pigs were born last night.'

'I don't see why he wants an axe,' said Fern who was only eight.

'Well,' said her mother, 'one of the pigs is a runt. It's very small and weak and it will never amount to anything. So your father has decided to do away with it.'

'Do away with it?' shrieked Fern. 'You mean kill it? Just because it's smaller than the others?'

from *Charlotte's Web* by E.B. White
(Hamish Hamilton, 1952).

◆ This is where the trouble begins.

It is an excellent opening: it has conflict and an urgent problem. Details that would have been flat if told in the narrative (Fern Arable, a farmer's daughter, was eight years old) are easily absorbed from the dialogue. It has a hook that makes the reader want to read on – what is going to happen to the runt?

Here is another conversational opening, full of movement, tension and conflict.

> 'Too many!' James shouted and slammed the door behind him.
>
> 'What?' said Will.
>
> 'Too many kids in this family, that's what. Just too many.' James stood fuming on the landing like a small, angry locomotive, then stumped across to the window-seat and stared into the garden. Will put aside his book and pulled up his legs to make room. 'I could hear all the yelling,' he said, chin on his knees.
>
> 'Wasn't anything,' James said, 'Just stupid Barbara again. Pick up this, don't touch that. And Mary joining in, twitter, twitter, twitter. You'd think this house was big enough but there's always people.'

from *The Dark is Rising* by Susan Cooper
(Chatto & Windus, 1966).

◆ This is where James finds something he can't stand.

Description plus
Scene-setting can be used as an opening if the description is

short and has an added extra. These two atmospheric openings are spiced by the words in my italics. The foreshadowed menace in each hook the reader.

It was bleak on Mottram Road under the Edge, the wooded hill of Alderley. Trees roared high in the darkness. If any people had cause to be out in the night, they kept their heads deep in their collars and their faces screwed blindly against the Pennine wind. And it was as well they did, *for among the trees something was happening that was not meant for human eyes.*

from *The Moon of Gomrath* by Alan Garner
(Collins, 1963).

◆ This is the day that was different.

Winter came early to the city that year. Josiah Davidson, emerging from the subway, shivered against the dank November rain which blew icily against his face and sent a trickle down the back of his neck. *He did not see the three boys in black jackets who moved out of a sheltered doorway and stalked him.*

from *The Young Unicorns* by Madeline l'Engle
(Gollancz, 1970).

◆ Another day that was different, also where the trouble begins.

The unexpected

Here are two openings that surprise the reader. With the first he asks, 'What on earth are these children doing?' The second is unusual enough to make him sit up and take notice and want to read on.

The frogs' legs were less appalling than the children had expected. They slid out of the tin with a plop, a slimy, grey-brown mass: very nasty, but not obviously legs. Martha was much relieved. She had expected pathetic little webbed feet at the ends.

'Seven and six for that lot!' said William with disgust. 'I jolly well hope they're worth it.'

Susie begin stirring the saucepan. The frogs' legs quickly disintegrated and merely served as a kind of thickening. The bird's wing floated suddenly to the top and Martha averted her eyes.

from *The Whispering Knights* by Penelope Lively
(Heinemann, 1971).

◆ Another day that was different.

The note said SOMEONE IN THIS CLASS IS A WITCH. It was written in capital letters in ordinary blue ballpoint and it had appeared between two of the geography books Mr Crossley was marking.

from *Witch Week* by Diana Wynne Jones (Macmillan, 1982).

◆ This is where the trouble begins.

Showing character
In the first, we see that Pansy is young, excited and scatterbrained, so we expect her to have misadventures. In the second, the situation is intriguing and a character like Sirius with such a temper is sure to stir things up. Two good openings with hooks.

That evening, Nana laid out Pansy's clothes to be packed on Pansy's bed. Her bathing dress and cap and folded water-wings looked almost as exciting and out of place in the middle of the counterpane as a bit of seeweed or a crab.

'Although you are only going for a fortnight . . .' Nana said.

'Ten whole days,' Pansy interrupted her, 'not counting tomorrow, Tuesday when we go and Saturday when we come back.'

'Although you're only going for ten whole days, I'm sending you with three lots of underclothes in case you have an accident.'

'What sort of accident?'

'I don't know and I hope you won't have one, but you're so scatter-brained you might do something silly like falling down in the sea, although goodness knows you're old enough now to be sensible . . .'

from *The Workhouse Child* by Geraldine Symons

(Macmillan, 1989).

◆ This is a day that was different.

The Dog Star stood beneath the Judgement Seat and raged. The green light of his fury fired the assembled faces viridian. It lit the underside of the roof-trees and turned their moist blue fruit to emerald.

'None of this is true,' he shouted. 'Why can't you believe me, instead of listening to *him*?' He blazed on the chief witness, a blue luminary from the Castor complex, firing him turquoise. The witness backed hastily out of range.

from *Dogsbody* by Diana Wynne Jones

(Macmillan, 1975).

◆ This is something the character can't stand.

CHECK YOUR FIRST PAGE

1. Does your story begin at a moment when something important is going to happen or has just happened?

2. Does the first paragraph grab the readers' attention and hook them?

3. Is it too static? There should be a sense of movement; to achieve this use active verbs rather than passive.

4. If there is no action, is there the promise of it?

5. Does it have a short first sentence? This will have more impact than a long one. Your first paragraph should be short too.

6. Does it pique readers' curiosity and make it unthinkable for them to lay the book down?

7. Have you introduced your main character? (This is not always possible but readers like to know for whom they should cheer.)

8. Make sure you haven't confused the reader by introducing more than two characters in the first few paragraphs.

9. Is there conflict or at least a problem?

10. Is there conversation or overheard thoughts?

None of these rules is set in stone, but they are a useful test.

Fig. 8. First page checklist.

Golden rules for openings

- Start at a moment of change in the key character's life.
- Make sure it is a change that will have consequences.
- Show the key character as soon as possible.
- Show him in action or in revealing conversation.
- Make the reader curious about what will happen next.

EXERCISES

Practise writing openings in different styles of about 150–250 words. Put them away for a day or two and come back to them: do they answer the questions on the Figure 8 checklist on page 77?

7

The Middle of the Book

Once you have started your book and hooked the reader, you have to go on, keeping up the interest, building towards the climax at the end. Make sure you have plenty for your characters to do.

HOLDING THE READER

At the start of a story the reader accepts easily and trustingly the information offered, but as the story progresses, unless there is internal logic, he may reject or question what you say. Everything must fit together.

Don't prepare the reader for something that isn't going to happen. Each thing you show him, the reader expects to be significant. For instance, in a film if you are shown a close-up of a toy left on a half-dark staircase, you expect it to trip someone. If you never see the toy again and no-one trips, you feel cheated.

Don't send your hero big-game-hunting after mice. In other words make sure the thing he is trying to achieve is important enough to bear the weight of your story.

Internal logic is especially important in fantasy. Magic must never be used as a cop-out to get the writer out of trouble, the ground must be laid for it, and you must keep within the parameters you lay down.

Scenes

Think in scenes, not chapters. Scenes are the building blocks from which you construct your chapters. A scene is a sequence of events like this:

1. Set up a situation.
2. Bring in conflict or problem which causes upset.
3. Reaction to upset.
4. Decision as to how to deal with problem/upset.
5. New situation which starts the next scene.

As was said in discussing outlines, what keeps the reader reading is conflict and complications. You cannot have too many of the two Cs. Look back to Chapter 4 for lists of conflict and complications.

There is one C of which you should be careful and that is coincidence. I know Dickens used them endlessly, but nowadays too many will disgust the reader. As a rule of thumb, you may use coincidence to get your characters into trouble, but *not* to get them out of it.

Always write in units of stimulus and response.

♦ Stimulus is something that happens outside your character:
♦ Response is the character's reaction.

This sounds obvious, but in the heat of the moment you can get things the wrong way round, as happens in an exaggerated fashion in *Alice Through the Looking Glass*:

> The White Queen runs around screaming. *Response.*
> A little while later she pricks her finger. *Stimulus.*

Rather, you want to write:

> The wind blew chill. *Stimulus.*
> John shivered and turned up his coat collar. *Response.*

Use emotion

Before you begin to write each scene ask yourself, what emotion do I want my reader to feel as he reads this? Do I want him to be apprehensive? Indignant? Scared? Intrigued? Happy at the outcome? Reader identification with the story demands emotion. When your character shows emotion, the reader feels it too.

The rule of three

Three has always been known as a 'magic' number and it can be useful to a writer. It is used in fairy tales because it establishes a pattern. Think how often three princes or princesses occur. Think of the three little pigs, the three bears, three blind mice. There are usually three tasks that the hero has to accomplish before he achieves his goal.

You can use this rule of three when your main character has to overcome an obstacle or solve a problem. The rule is that he fails twice and succeeds the third time.

- ◆ If he were to succeed the first time, it would be too easy and there would be no tension.
- ◆ If he succeeds the second time there is some tension but it is still too easy.

◆ Succeeding the third time is just right.

If you were to make it the fourth time it would be boring, the reader's eyes would glaze over.

With characters, as the proverb says, two's company and three's a crowd, but if you have three characters interacting you have more opportunity for conflict than with only two.

What does the hero fear?

In the character chart (Figure 7), one of the things it was suggested you ought to know about your main character is – what is he afraid of? You can use the answer to this question to create a dramatic situation if you make him face this fear. For instance, if he is afraid of heights, you ensure that the only way he can rescue his friend is to climb to the top of a building.

Remember, the character's intention + the reader's anticipation = suspense. Tension is created by the reader's identification with the character in jeopardy.

DIALOGUE

Children's books need lots of conversation, even more than in adult books. (We looked at the main purposes of dialogue in Chapter 5.) If you aim to have 50% of your book in dialogue you will be on the right lines. Enid Blyton was good at dialogue (although hers is dated now); she even used dialogue to describe places and things. If your character is alone, use interior monologue, which counts as dialogue, or let him confide in his pet dog.

In dialogue, disagreement makes for the illusion of movement: too much assent becomes static and is dull. All dialogue must be there because the character cares about it, not just because the writer wants to say it, and each speech must suit the character who says it.

The ubiquitous 'said'

In two-handed conversations, it is not always necessary to have *said* phrases for every remark. Do without them wherever you can: it quickens the pace of the story.

- Don't entirely despise the word *said*. It is the mark of the amateur to strive for as many different ways as possible of attributing speech. You cannot laugh/grin/smile a remark. Not '"Here we are," she smiled,' but '"Here we are," she said with a smile.'
- Even better than a *said* phrase is an *action* phrase that shows who is making the remark and what they are doing while speaking. As in, 'Come off it.' Brian shut the gate. 'You're not really going to tell Felicity, are you?'
- You can put emotion into your attributions by using adverbs, *hotly*, *kindly*, *crossly*, *fiercely* and so on but if it is not there in the speech, you are wasting your time. Only use adverbs to modify your *said* phrase if the way the speech is said is not implied by the content. If you write, ' "Go away!" he said,' you expect the remark to be angry, so there is no need to add 'crossly'. But in ' "Go away," she said softly, her voice breaking,' the implication is different and the adverb is justified.
- Don't overdo dialects or foreign accents. It is better to indicate the fact that someone is speaking a foreign language by translating foreign idioms into English and

using the foreign word order. (Poirot on television is a perfect example of this.) In the case of dialect, use an occasional dialect expression and every so often remind the reader by using a phrase like, 'he said in his rich Devon burr' or 'he said in his sharp Cockney accent.'

♦ Swearing is commonplace among children nowadays, but editors are wary of it. You can get around this by making up equivalents, or saying something like,

'He used a word that made Hermione say *Ron!*' (J.K. Rowling in *The Prisoner of Azkaban*); or even, 'He used some choice words that would have shocked his Granny.'

Scene-setting

Just as the two Cs are important in keeping the reader hooked, the two Vs are vital when you are writing – your writing must be vivid and visual.

When you are going to write an important scene, collect words you might use when describing the event. If you are going to write about a shipwreck, list the words you would use to describe the sea, the wind, the sounds, the colours of the stormy sky and so on. With your list, you have a selection of words to choose from as you write in white-hot passion.

Remember to keep description short unless it is interspersed with action or conveyed in dialogue. Make your descriptions vivid and interesting. Here is William Mayne in *Sand* (Hamish Hamilton, 1964), describing a shirt on a cold and frosty morning.

The shirt was made of cold cloth and frozen buttons. It lay on Ainsley's bed like a drift of snow. The cold spring wind blew the curtains and moaned under the door. Ainsley stroked the shirt. It had been starched with ice.

Don't forget to use senses other than sight.

◆ Smell evokes strong images in readers' minds, things like *wood smoke*, *toast burning*, *salt and sea*, *hot coffee*.
◆ Taste is important too: children love to read about what people eat. Ann Fine, in a recent article on Enid Blyton, says she read Blyton's books solidly for five days and put on six pounds! Another writer told me she blamed her sweet tooth on Blyton's tree that grew sweets. Today's children revel in J.K. Rowling's invented confectionery delights.

> Bertie Bott's Every Flavour Beans, Drooble's Best Blowing Gum, Chocolate Frogs, Pumpkin Pasties, Cauldron Cakes, Liquorice Wands and a number of strange things Harry had never seen in his life. Not wanting to miss anything, he got some of everything . . .

from *Harry Potter and the Philosopher's Stone*
(Bloomsbury, 1997).

◆ For sound, use onomatopoeia. Made-up words like *thwack*, *whizz*, *boing*, *splat* imitate the sound they are describing. Real words like *whisper*, *murmur*, *swish*, *squeak*, *rustle* do a similar job.

Settings

This is the place in which your story is set, the 'where' we talked about when considering plot development. No long descriptions of the main character's home or school, unless they are very unusual. Feed in the description in small doses. Ann Fine says, 'Description has a mego factor of 10 for the young reader: mego being P.J. O'Rourke's way of saying, My Eyes Glaze Over.'

In an action sequence, for maximum effect, choose a place where things can go wrong. If it's a chase, use a cul-de-sac; if it's a fight, put them near a cliff edge and so on. Remember, character's danger + reader's anticipation = suspense.

WRITER'S BLOCK

Don't let this frighten you, it is just a grand name for getting stuck. The writer-father in one of Diana Wynne Jones's books describes it:

> You haven't a thought in your head, or if you have you somehow can't get it down on paper or if you *do* manage to put something down it goes all small and boring and doesn't lead anywhere.

Is it a question of verifying a fact?

If possible, write on leaving a gap and look it up later. If it's something you must see, go and look or consult an expert.

Use the Internet. www.google.com finds answers to almost anything.

What happens next?

If, in spite of your outline, you can't think what happens next, get up from your desk and have some thinking time. Do something with your hands that leaves your mind free. Alternatively, if you know a scene that is coming soon, write that and find your link later. You may even find you don't need a link and you will have made a jump cut.

I've written myself into a corner!

Make a list of six things that could happen even if they are improbable. See if one would work if you made a minor change in an earlier chapter.

Whose story is it?

If a minor character seems to be elbowing the main character out of his rightful place, ask yourself:

- Should it be *his* story?
- Are you using the right viewpoint?
- Should you be looking through another character's eyes?

Sometimes you have to be stern and cut some of the secondary character's business: the hero ought to have the best lines and the important action.

It doesn't ring true!

If your story seems flat, ask yourself:

- Can the reader visualise what is going on?
- Is there enough emotion?
- Is your main character too good to be true?
- Is there enough conflict?
- Have you made the reader care what happens to your characters?
- Does he love the hero and hate the villain?
- Do you? If you don't feel passionately about your characters, no-one else will.

There's not enough atmosphere

◆ Have you remembered to use all the senses?

◆ Does the reader know what season it is, what the weather is like?

◆ Are your descriptions vivid enough?

◆ Is your language punchy enough?

It still won't come right

If all these solutions fail, write on anyway: write almost anything and then suddenly you may find yourself on the right track again with only two or three pages to discard.

Sometimes you can breathe life into a story by introducing a new character.

Have you written too small?

It is important to give enough words to big scenes. If they are over in a flash, the reader will think them unimportant. The tenser the situation for your key character, the more words you should give it. You need plenty of detail when your character is in danger or a tight spot. The reader wants to know how he feels, what he sees, hears, smells and so on. P.G. Wodehouse said:

> The success of every novel depends on one or two high spots. Say to yourself, 'Which are my big scenes?' and get every ounce of juice out of them.

EXERCISES

1. Make a list of the words you might want to use if you were going to describe a visit to a fairground.

2. A twelve year old boy is entering a house he has never visited before. Describe the way it smells to him.

3. His sister is fourteen. Would she notice the same smells? If not, what would strike her?

4. These two go out into the garden. What would he notice? What would she notice?

5. If your eight year old hero is afraid of the dark, how would you use this in a story?

$$\left(8\right)$$

The End

The ending of your book is as important as the beginning. You want to leave your reader satisfied, you want him to recommend your book to his friends and you want to make him anxious to read your next book. The thing that your reader remembers best is the thing he reads last. If he is disappointed by the ending, however good the rest of the book, he will consider the story has failed.

PAYOFF TIME

As you approach the end of your book, the pace should quicken and the issue should be fined down. Then you come to the climax, the payoff towards which all the writing you have done has been leading.

The climax should be the biggest scene in the whole book. In it, your main character will triumph or be vanquished, achieve his object or fail. Heighten the suspense by making the reader uncertain which way things will go in the final test. Pile on the tension by having a black moment when all seems lost just before success is achieved.

The best known ending for children's stories is, 'and they all lived happily ever after'. We seldom use those very words except in fairy tales, but they encapsulate the feeling we try to create. Young readers want to believe that however exciting, amazing or dangerous an adventure has been, everything has finally been sorted out and all is well.

Children's stories should end happily or at least with hope. Richard Peck, who writes for teenagers, said of his readers:

> They are not looking for reality, they are looking for hope and if you do not have a happy ending you had better do some fast talking.

So, if to be artistically right your story cannot have a happy ending, at least make it upbeat with the possibility of later triumph, like the ending of *Gone With the Wind* – 'I'll think of it all tomorrow . . . After all, tomorrow is another day.'

Some stories end at the moment of triumph, but more often the climax is followed by a gentle incident, a grace note full of warmth that rounds the story off and allows the reader, who has been holding his breath, to breathe again.

◆ *Watchpoint*: Don't be so anxious to write 'the end' that you hurry over the climax and leave your readers feeling let down.

Some useful endings

Happy-ever-after endings
Having told the readers in a few lines what happened to each of the characters, John Masefield ended *The Midnight Folk* thus:

> You may be sure that there is no more witchcraft in the house, nothing but peace and mirth all day and at night,

peace; the owls crying, crickets chirping and all sorts of fun going on among the Midnight Folk. (Macmillan, 1927)

Going home to safety

This is another type of ending beloved of children. In *Arabel's Raven* by Joan Aiken, after many adventures, Arabel is pulling Mortimer, her raven, home on her little red cart.

Mr Jones was inside and had just made a pot of tea. When he saw them coming in the front gate, he poured out an eggcupful for Mortimer. They all sat round the kitchen table and had tea. Mortimer had several eggcups full and as for Arabel, she made up for all the meals she had missed while Mortimer had been lost. (BBC Publications, 1972)

Maurice Sendak used this type of ending brilliantly in *Where the Wild Things Are* so that Max, having been half way round the world, and romped and rampaged with the wild things, arrives home to the safety of his bedroom and finds that his supper is still hot.

Almost sad but . . .

Endings must be artistically right even if they are not quite what the reader expects. In the film of *The Witches* the boy who has been turned into a mouse is changed back. This annoyed Roald Dahl because it destroyed the point he was making. The boy, whose only kin was his grandmother, was pleased to be a mouse because his lifespan would match hers. He had no desire to be alone when she died. Dahl's skilful writing ensures the reader recognises this. His ending is more satisfying than that of the film.

'It will be a triumph my darling! A colossal, unbeatable triumph! We shall do it entirely by ourselves, just you and me. That will be our work for the rest of our lives!'

My grandmother picked me up off the table and kissed me on the nose. 'Oh goodness me, we're going to be busy these next few weeks and months and years!' she cried.

'I think we are,' I said. 'But what fun and excitement it's going to be.'

'You can say that again!' my grandmother cried, giving me another kiss. 'I can't wait to get started.'

from *The Witches* by Roald Dahl   (Cape, 1983).

The ending that holds a new beginning
The open end is often used when the writer plans a sequel, but it can be used to foreshadow another adventure that the reader can create in his own head (the Dahl example does this too.)

'Thank goodness that's over,' said Timothy.

'Yes,' said Nancy with a new look in her eyes, 'and only ten days gone after all. An awful ten days, but worth it to save Mother. And now at last we're free to start stirring things up. We'll hoist the skull and crossbones again the moment we've had our grub. We'll get things moving without wasting a minute . . .'

Timothy sat up suddenly. 'Oh look here, I'm all for a quiet life after this.'

'Well you won't exactly have one,' said Nancy, 'Not yet, you can't expect it. Not with the Swallows coming and Uncle Jim and five whole weeks of the holidays still to go.'

from *The Picts and the Martyrs* by Arthur Ransome
(Cape, 1943).

Sharing a secret

Tom is saying goodbye to an old lady who, as a young girl, was his friend on a different time scale. Aunt Gwen doesn't know this although the reader does. The secret knowledge gives the ending its warmth.

> 'Goodbye Mrs Bartholomew,' said Tom shaking hands with stiff politeness, 'and thank you very much for having me.'
>
> 'I shall look forward to our meeting again,' said Mrs Bartholomew, equally primly.
>
> Tom went down the attic stairs. Then, at the bottom, he hesitated, turned impulsively and ran up again, two at a time, to where Hatty Bartholomew still stood.
>
> Afterwards, Aunt Gwen tried to describe to her husband that second parting. 'He ran up to her and they hugged each other as if they'd known each other for years, instead of only having met this morning. Of course, Mrs Bartholomew's such a shrunken little old woman, she's hardly bigger than Tom anyway: but you know, he put his arms right round her and he hugged her as if she were a little girl.'

from *Tom's Midnight Garden* by Philippa Pearce

(OUP, 1958).

Endings that come full circle

The books about the orphan wizard Harry Potter all start with our hero having a terrible time with his horrible Muggle (non-magic) relations. They end with Harry, having had a wonderful year at Hogwarts, going back to them in an upbeat frame of mind.

> It was Uncle Vernon still purple-faced, still moustached, still looking furious at the nerve of Harry, carrying an owl

in a cage in a station full of ordinary people. Behind him stood Aunt Petunia and Dudley, looking terrified at the very sight of Harry . . . .

Harry hung back for a last word with Ron and Hermione.

'See you over the summer then.'

'Hope you have – er – a good holiday,' said Hermione, looking uncertainly after Uncle Vernon, shocked that anyone could be so unpleasant.

'Oh I will,' said Harry and they were surprised at the grin that was spreading over his face. 'They don't know we're not allowed to use magic at home. I'm going to have a lot of fun with Dudley this summer.'

from *Harry Potter and the Philosopher's Stone*

(Bloomsbury, 1997).

'This is called a telephone number,' he told Ron scribbling it twice, tearing the parchment in two and handing it to them. 'I told your Dad how to use a telephone last summer, he'll know. Call me at the Dursley's, OK? I can't stand another two months with only Dudley to talk to.'

'Your Aunt and Uncle will be proud, though, won't they?' said Hermione, as they got off the train and joined the crowd thronging towards the enchanted barrier. 'When they hear what you've done this year?'

'Proud?' said Harry. 'Are you mad? All those times I could have died and I didn't manage it? They'll be furious . . .'

And together they walked back through the gateway to the Muggle world.

from *Harry Potter and the Chamber of Secrets*

(Bloomsbury, 1998).

'It's a letter from my Godfather,' said Harry cheerfully.

'Godfather,' spluttered Uncle Vernon. 'You haven't got a Godfather.'

'Yes I have,' said Harry brightly. 'He was my mum and dad's best friend. He's a convicted murderer, but he's broken out of wizard prison and he's on the run. He likes to keep in touch with me, though . . . keep up with my news . . . check that I'm happy . . .'

And grinning broadly at the look of horror on Uncle Vernon's face, Harry set off towards the station exit, Hedwig* rattling along in front of him, for what looked like a much better summer than the last.

Harry's owl

from *Harry Potter and the Prisoner of Azkaban* (Bloomsbury 1999) all three by J.K. Rowling.

It is worth spending some time on getting your ending just right in the same way that you worked at your opening, for as H.E. Bates said on this subject, 'A story is like a horse race, the start and the finish are what count most.'

EXERCISES

Check how the endings are handled in books for your chosen age group. Would you have ended the stories like that? Can you think of better ways to do it?

9

Writing a Non-Fiction Book

Non-fiction books sell well. Publishers want new titles for the recreational market and information books for the educational market. Schools require children to do a lot of project work, and for this they borrow from public libraries and the school library, so sales are good. I am still getting PLR (Public Lending Right fees) from non-fiction books written and published over ten years ago even though the books are now out of print.

WHAT SORT OF SUBJECTS?

Many of you will have favourite subjects to do with your work or your hobbies about which you could write a book for children.

Check the subjects covered in the National Curriculum to see whether any of these mesh with your interests, but be aware many writers will also do this, so other subjects may be more acceptable.

A recent trend in the information book market has been to use humour in tackling certain subjects. It's the spoonful of sugar that makes the medicine go down. Have a look at the Horrible History series in which Terry Deary deals with subjects like *Cut-throat Celts* and *Measly Middle Ages*. Oxford University Press have introduced Scratch 'n' Sniff books in their Smelly Old History series with names like *Tudor Odours* by Mary Dobson.

WHO IS THE BOOK INTENDED FOR?

Information books, like fiction, should be precisely aimed at a particular age group. Don't be vague and say – anyone from eight to eighty: it sounds good, but it simply will not do. Suppose that you decide to write a book about BREAD, you would handle it differently for each age group.

1. For 5–7 year olds

For this age group, the book should be simple with a few sentences on each page. Begin with wheat growing in a field, go on to the farmer harvesting, then the grain being made into flour at a mill. Then show the baker making dough with the addition of yeast, then show the loaves being put in the oven. The cooked loaves will be shown being wrapped and taken to the supermarket; a mother and child will choose the loaf they want. Finally the family will be seen eating toast or sandwiches.

Write the text that goes with the scenes you have visualised and suggest that brightly coloured illustrations will complement your text. Don't say exactly what you want drawn – leave that to the artist and the editor.

2. 8–11 year olds

Use the same basic pattern for this age group, but for them each topic would be a complete chapter and you offer more information.

In the first chapter, besides showing wheat growing, you explain where it grows and talk about its cultivation.

In the chapter on harvesting, you might discuss the methods of the past when a team of men used scythes, stooked the sheaves, took them to the barn with a horse and cart and then threshed the grain. You could compare that with today when a combine harvester driven by one man does all these tasks. You could discuss grain yields per acre and mention the farmer's enemies – bugs, blight, drought and so on.

When you write about milling, you could compare old-fashioned windmills and watermills with modern mills; you might discuss the difference between white and wholemeal flour and point out the change in fashion.

Finally, you would suggest that this book could be illustrated with more detailed drawings or photographs and charts.

RESEARCH

You need to do two kinds of research for non-fiction: your market and your subject.

Market research

This is vital for information books. You need to find out if the subject has already been covered. In the library check *Books in Print* and check on the Internet. If it has, you can still write your book, but plan to tackle it from a different angle.

A study of publishers' catalogues and a look at what is on the library shelves will help you select the most suitable publisher. Ask at the public library for the Spring and Autumn numbers of the magazine *The Bookseller*. These are large volumes in which publishers advertise their forthcoming books. You will see which publishers have series: look for one into which your book might be slotted. You will also be able to see if there is anything similar coming up.

Researching the text

As well as reading as many books on the subject as you can, do practical research. In the case of bread:

- Talk to a farmer who grows wheat.
- Go and visit a mill – a modern one and an old windmill for comparison.
- Telephone the publicity department of a large bread company and find out which types of bread are most popular. They will be glad to supply you with photos in return for a promised acknowledgement.
- Use your imagination to find fresh angles on the subject.
- Talk to children and find out what they know about bread and ask them what they would like to know.

APPROACHING A PUBLISHER

Don't write the whole book on spec and send out a finished manuscript. *Do* write a book proposal and send it to the publisher of your choice.

Why a book proposal? Because it is the professional way to sell a non-fiction book. The reasons it works are:

1. The editor can read it and make a quick decision: this is

advantageous for both of you – the editor saves time, and you don't waste time writing something that is not wanted.

2. If the editor likes your idea, you will be called in for a discussion and the book can be shaped to suit the publisher's list. Again advantageous to both you and the publisher.

COMPILING A BOOK PROPOSAL

A book proposal has three parts – an introduction, an outline, and a sample chapter. Along with these, you will send a covering letter.

Introduction

This should include:

1. An overview that sets out in a few paragraphs your subject and your aim. It also says for whom the book is intended.
2. Why *you* are writing it. Couch this in the third person, as in, 'Kitty Fisher has a diploma in Home Economics and is extremely interested in bread production . . .'
3. Why you are offering it to *this* publisher. 'Kitty Fisher has read with interest the books you published on BACON and CHEESE and feels that a book on BREAD would fit into your *Food on the Table* series.'
4. Your market and who will buy it. 'Children are increasingly doing projects on "green" subjects and although there is a book on some aspects of BREAD in Blank & Dash's *Kitchen Cupboard* series, this book will cover the subject more fully and will look at the historical angle, comparing the past with the present and it will show that bread made from flour obtained from

organically grown wheat is better for health and for the environment. It is intended that this book will be interesting enough for private reading and informative enough for teachers to use in class.'

5. How you envisage the book. 'Like others in your *Food on the Table* series, the text is envisaged interspersed with coloured photographs, black and white drawings and charts.'

Outline

This is a chapter by chapter breakdown of the proposed book. Put each chapter on a separate page; if possible, give each chapter a catchy title then give a brief description of what will be in the chapter. Write about the *chapter* not the *subject*; write in the present tense. For example:

Chapter 1 *Bread out of the Ground*

This chapter shows how the wheat is grown from seed to ear. It describes different methods of cultivation, comparing the past with the present. The areas of the world where wheat is grown are enumerated. The farmer's enemies, from bad weather to pests are discussed

. . .

Sample chapter

This is your chance to show:

◆ how you will tackle the subject
◆ what your style is like
◆ the tone of the book.

You can choose any chapter as your sample for a non-fiction book. (Compare this with sample chapters of fiction in Chapter 11.)

All this should be well laid out, immaculately typed on A4 paper in double spacing. Don't staple or clip pages together, but number them and put the whole thing in a labelled folder.

Your covering letter

Keep this short. Simply say you are enclosing a proposal for a non-fiction book for X year olds on the subject of bread. All the information about your book should be in the proposal so it is a waste of time to repeat it in the letter. Don't forget to enclose a stamped addressed envelope for reply or return of MS if it is not suitable. (See Chapter 11 for length of probable reaction time.)

Illustrations

These may safely be left to the editor to choose. However, if during your research you collected photographs which you think might be suitable, mention them but don't send them at this stage. If you are an artist as well as a writer, send only one illustration as a sample, and be sure it's a photocopy: don't send original artwork.

BIOGRAPHIES

If you want to write the life story of a particular hero or heroine of yours, try to find an existing series into which your chosen character will fit. Look at the output of educational publishers as well as general children's publishers for this type of book.

Sometimes the entire life is written and sometimes it is only the subject's childhood that is wanted. If you cannot find a series, it might be worth approaching publishers and suggesting one. Do the book proposal for your first choice, and in your letter suggest names of further possible subjects.

STEP-BY-STEP BOOKS

If you are skilled at crafts and can explain clearly, step by step, how to make something, there is always room for a good book of this kind.

Social skills can be presented in step-by-step 'how to . .' books too: how to write letters, how to behave at the dentist, how to look after your guinea pig and so on.

ACTIVITY BOOKS

This is the sort of book that keeps children quiet on journeys – a mixture of puzzles, riddles, quizzes and pencil and paper games. Activity books can be tied to certain times of year. Things to do on the beach, special Christmas or Easter activity books are obvious, but try to be original. How about Halloween or Valentine activity books for instance?

JOKE BOOKS

Before you embark on one of these, take a look at those available. The jokes are often corny, the sort you get in Christmas crackers; the sort that are greeted with groans by adults but loved by children. The way to make a joke book saleable is to collect your jokes around a theme – something like *101 Chicken Jokes*, perhaps.

Activity and joke books are best offered to paperback

publishers rather than hardback houses, although b small press (website: www.bsmall.co.uk) do activity books.

Golden rules for non-fiction books

◆ Research meticulously and imaginatively.

◆ Check every fact: children tend to take the printed word as gospel so you owe it to them to be accurate. If you get one fact wrong, reviewers will be down on you like a ton of bricks.

◆ Choose a subject about which you are enthusiastic. If it bores you, it will bore your readers.

◆ Be even-handed and fair. If there is controversy about your subject, you must show both sides of the question.

EXERCISES

1. Make a list of subjects that interest you enough to make you want to write a book on them.

2. Write part 1 (Introduction) and part 2 (Outline) for a book proposal for a non-fiction book on a subject of your choice either for 5–7 year olds or 8–11 year olds.

3. Make a list of publishers who have series of non-fiction books and check out their required lengths.

4. Check on activity books and joke books and see if you can find a gap in the market.

10

Revising – Getting it Right

There are three parts to writing a book:

◆ Getting it written.
◆ Getting it right.
◆ Getting it published.

You have achieved the first part and have written THE END. You feel a great sense of achievement – and rightly so. Now is the time for the second part.

When you were writing you were Mr Creator and inside the story. Now you must change hats and become Mr Critic. You must look at your story from the outside as you revise and polish.

Don't rush into this: wait a week or two (some writers recommend a month at least) in order to distance yourself from it. Do another piece of writing, perhaps the preliminary work on your next book. Then you are ready to start the revision.

CUTTING – DUMPING DEAD WORDS

Cutting is vital: it is like raking the slag out of a fire to make it burn more brightly. So get out your red pen and be ruthless:

- Cut any section that is not relevant to your plot and your theme. As you read, ask yourself what is the point of this scene? This paragraph? This sentence? This word?
- Cut unnecessary words and phrases. Have you said obvious things like – 'He put his hat on *his head*.'?
  You need only say where he put his hat if it is somewhere other than his head – 'He put his hat *on the table*.'
  He fell *down*. (How many people fall up?)
- Check for repetition. Repetition of a certain kind is good in books for the very young, but for older children the overuse of the same word in one paragraph is clumsy and calls for you to find alternatives.
- Are there too many adjectives? Do you really need them all? Three adjectives to a noun is overkill. Two is possible, one is better, or could you do without any? Be careful of tautological (saying the same thing twice) phrases like *glowing* ember; his face was ashen *grey*; he kept a *daily* journal.
- Declare war on qualifiers like *very*, *quite*, *rather*, and *so* (especially *ever so*). Using them usually means you need something stronger. Instead of 'he was very tired,' try 'he was exhausted.' 'She was quite nice', try 'she was pleasant.' (Don't ever use *nice*, it's another empty word, find a better one.) Beware of words like *basically*, *actually*, *literally*: you can nearly always strike them out unless they are used in the conversation of a certain kind of person.
- Are there too many adverbs? You only need them if the way a thing is said or done is against the usual tendency of the verb.
- Replace long words with short ones if they are as good. Don't say 'proceed' if you can use 'go'.

- Use the active voice rather than the passive wherever possible. 'The boy carried the book' not 'The book was carried by the boy'.
- Are there any dull bits? Cut them or rewrite them.
- Have you told the reader something you could have shown in a scene?
- Be specific rather than general. Not, 'the creature was trembling,' but 'the horse trembled.' In these three phrases:

   A number of people think . . .

   Several scientists agree . . .

   Five biologists stated . . .

   each succeeding phrase is better than the one above it because it is more specific.

   In the same way don't say 'he took the train . . .' say 'he caught the 9.31 to Norwich . . .' Specific details lend authority to statements.
- Are your sentences too long? Too short? Are they varied? Break up paragraphs that are too long because they contain more than one idea.
- Check for consistency. Make sure you haven't given the heroine green eyes on page 20 and grey ones on page 42.

Checking your characterisation

We *cut* to improve the pace of the book, and we *add or rewrite* to improve characterisation, remembering how important characterisation is.

- Make a list of your main characters and give each of them three adjectives that sum up your vision of the person. Now go through your book and make sure that every action and every speech by these characters is in line with these three adjectives.

♦ Do you need all the characters? If you find there is a minor character who doesn't have much to say or do, could you combine her with another? This is often possible in a group of children of similar ages and background – instead of having the heroine's friends Milly and Elaine, could you cut one and give her lines and actions to the other? P.G. Wodehouse said that he classed his characters as if they were salaried actors and he was on a budget.

♦ Are there any scenes where there are a number of people, several of whom say nothing and do nothing? If so, do you need them all to be there? If you must have them, give them something to say or do.

Check the dialogue

If you have followed the advice on dialogue in Chapters 5 and 7, your dialogue should be in good shape, but it is worth having a fresh look to make sure it is concise and meaningful:

♦ Sometimes instead of the throat-clearing openings that occur in real conversation – Good morning. Hullo, how nice to see you. The weather's nice isn't it? – you can write something like:

> He exchanged greetings with Mike's mother, then when he and Mike were alone he said, 'Did you find out about the ghost?'

♦ Have you started speeches with, 'Well . . .'? This is an empty opening word you can almost always do without.

♦ Are any of your speeches really long? A speech of two or three sentences is the most that a person usually gets out before someone interrupts or it is someone else's turn to speak.

◆ Is there enough dialogue? Children's stories should be almost 50% dialogue.

◆ Are there any places where you could use dialogue instead of narrative?

Go back to the beginning

The part of your book that will probably need most reworking is the first chapter. Now you have completed the book, you know your characters better than when you began, you will see things in your first chapter you want to alter. Make sure you have begun your story in the right place. Remember what was said in Chapter 6: you must hook your readers on the first page and keep them so interested that they cannot bear to put the book down.

Common faults

Here is a list compiled by a publisher's reader of common faults. If you have followed the lessons and done your revision well, your story should have none of these, but check:

◆ theme too ordinary
◆ slow beginning
◆ wrong viewpoint character
◆ too many characters
◆ shallow characterisation
◆ too much trivia
◆ too much purple prose
◆ stilted dialogue
◆ too little dialogue
◆ too much generalisation
◆ irrelevant episodes

◆ lack of conflict
◆ flat ending
◆ cop-out ending.

Golden rule for revision

I cannot do better than quote Marjorie Allingham who said:

> I write everything four times: once to get my meaning
> down, once to put in everything I left out, once to take
> out everything that is unnecessary, and once to make the
> whole thing sound as if I had only just thought of it.

CHOOSING A TITLE

You may already have found your title, but if you haven't
now is the time to do so. A good title for a book or story can
help you sell it. It must intrigue the potential reader and make
him pick it off the shelf; it must sum up the story without
giving the whole plot away. Finally, it should be easy to say
and to remember. Something like *The Illustrated Mum*
(Jacqueline Wilson).

Although Dickens used *Oliver Twist*, *David Copperfield* and
Nicholas Nickelby as titles, nowadays it is better not to use
the main character's name on its own. But, if it is in
juxtaposition with something that raises a question in the
reader's mind, using a name can be good. *James and the
Giant Peach* (Roald Dahl), *Harriet the Spy* (Louise
Fitzhugh), *Mrs Frisby and the Rats of NIMH* (Robert
O'Brien) are all best-selling titles. Once your character is
established, it is a positive advantage to use the name in
sequels – *Paddington and the . . .* (Michael Bond), *Ramona*

and . . . (Beverly Cleary), *Harry Potter and the . . .* (J.K. Rowling).

Abstractions are currently popular for adult novels such as *Destiny* (Sally Beauman), *Possession* (A.S. Byatt): but don't use them for children. They like titles that conjure up pictures – *Warlock at the Wheel* (Diana Wynne Jones), *The Iron Man* (Ted Hughes), *The House on the Brink* (John Gordon).

Titles that tell where the story takes place are effective: *Treasure Island* (R.L. Stevenson), *The Children of Green Knowe* (Lucy Boston), *The House in Norham Gardens* (Penelope Lively). If the location is unusual, so much the better: *In the Night Kitchen* (Maurice Sendak), *Through the Dolls' House Door* (Jane Gardam), *At the Back of the North Wind* (George MacDonald).

Alliteration is attractive: *Harrow and Harvest* (Barbara Willard), *Cart and Cwidder* (Diana Wynne Jones), *The Wind in the Willows* (Kenneth Grahame). Titles should flow and trip off the tongue. Consider those with the choriambic metre: *King Solomon's Mines* (H. Rider Haggard), *The Box of Delights* (John Masefield), *A Little Princess* (F. Hodgson Burnett), *The Lord of the Rings* (J.R.R. Tolkien).

There was a fashion in America a few years ago for long titles: *Tell Me That You Love Me, Junie Moon* (Marjorie Kellogg), *If I Love You, Am I Trapped Forever?* (M.E. Kerr) but they are much less used in the UK – think of the problems for the graphic designer who had to get *The High Rise Glorious Skittleskat Roarious Sky Pie Angel Food Cake* (Nancy Willard) onto a book spine! Five or six words are about the maximum you should consider, and a short title is more easily remembered.

Certain words are surefire child magnets. You can probably think of any number of titles containing one of these magic words: *Secret, Magic, Mystery, Enchanted, Ghost, Witch, Wizard, Dragon, Dinosaur.*

A final note: there is no copyright in titles. If the title that fits your book has already been used, you can use it again, but if it is a recent book, it may cause confusion and if it is a very famous book, it is inadvisable. However you can always put on the first page of your MS, 'Working title – *Gone With the Wind*', and be prepared to be guided by your publisher.

PREPARING YOUR MS

After all this cutting and polishing, your MS will be a mess and will have to be retyped, but you would have done that anyway to make sure your book is immaculate. Editors can tell a lot by the way a typescript looks so you should aim to make yours as professional as possible:

- ◆ Check carefully for correct spelling, grammar and punctuation. These do matter: nowadays copy editing is expensive and editors look for MSS that need little or no work to be done on them.
- ◆ When setting out dialogue, note that the punctuation mark should come *inside* the closing inverted commas, not outside.
- ◆ The title page should give the author's name, address and

telephone number as well as the title and author together with the appropriate number of words. See below for wordage calculation. A model cover sheet is shown in Figure 9.

◆ Although block setting is the current fashion for letters, in a book MS, paragraphs should be indented 5 or 10 spaces.

◆ Extra line spaces should not be left between paragraphs or dialogue other than to indicate a change of location, time lapse, viewpoint shift or similar.

◆ Each time you start a new piece of dialogue or the phrase that introduces new dialogue, you should start a new paragraph indented.

◆ Your MS must be typed on A4 paper in double spacing. Always use white paper.

◆ Margins should be 1½–2″ on the left and at least 1″ on the right.

◆ Leave 1½″ at the top and the foot of the page.

◆ Don't justify the right hand margin (this makes word counting hard for the printer or compositor).

◆ Number pages continuously throughout the book, not starting again at 1 for each chapter.

◆ If your machine can provide a header, use the title (or part of it) and your name. The header for this book, for example, was *Writing for Children/Cleaver*. This is useful in case part of the book becomes separated from the whole.

◆ Start each chapter on a new page. If your chapters are not titled, centre *Chapter 1*, turn up at least eight lots of double spacing and begin. (Editors like this space for writing comments on the setting for the printer.)

◆ If your chapters are named, set the heading out like this:

A children's book of approximately 8,000 words

THE MAGIC BICYCLE

by   Emma   Payne

Emma Payne
Holly Cottage
Ashen Market
Beds.

Tel: 01973 642 973

Fig. 9. Model cover sheet.

Chapter 1   MARGARET LEAVES HOME

At the end of each chapter, centre some dots.

. . .   .

but at the end of the final chapter put

. . .   THE END   . . .

Under that put © and your name and the year to establish your copyright. It is a good idea to put your name and address again on the last page of your MS near the foot.

◆ Do not clip pages together or fasten or bind them in any way.

◆ Put the whole thing in a labelled folder marked with your name and address and the title. Put a rubber band round it to keep it secure.

◆ Make sure you have a copy of the MS. Even if you have it on disk, a hard copy is important because machines can go wrong and disks can corrupt. Also you will need your typescript if an editor rings up and says, 'about the passage on page 32 . . .'.

To estimate word count

1. Count the number of words in 10 complete lines (not short dialogue lines or the final line of a paragraph).
2. Divide by 10 to get average number of words per line, e.g. 11 words per line.
3. Multiply by the total number of lines in a full page, e.g. 11 × 28 = 308.
4. Multiply this figure by total number of pages, e.g. 308 × 180 = 55,440 words.
5. Round this down and call it 55,000 words approx.

Publishers these days are increasingly willing to accept a computer word count. If you use this method, call it 9,346 words (computer count).

Publishers' pet hates

◆ manuscripts on coloured paper
◆ tattered MSS that have obviously been the rounds
◆ numerous alterations in ink
◆ uncut fanfold paper
◆ chapters fastened together with dressmaker's pins
◆ faded typewriter ribbons that can hardly be read and faint dot matrix printing
◆ typing in single spacing
◆ handwritten MSS
◆ fancy type faces and type smaller than 12 point.

EXERCISES

1. Take a story (or a chapter from a book) that you have written and cut 500 words from it. To be able to do this is important. I was once told by an editor that if I condensed the first three pages of a story into two paragraphs she would buy it.

2. Take a page from one of your stories and cut out every adjective. Now put back only those you find essential. See how many words you have saved and whether the sense is clearer.

3. Do the same with another page this time deleting all adverbs.

4. Check the titles of some of the children's books on your shelves. Decide which titles are most effective and why.

(11)

Finding a Publisher

Your book is written, you have subjected it to an exhaustive revision, you have prepared a fair copy and you feel it is ready to go out and seek its fortune. You have done your market research and decided which publishers are most likely to be interested. How do you approach these publishers?

SENDING OUT YOUR MS

If yours is a book for younger children, a picture book or a series book of less than 7,000 words, you can send the complete MS. If it is a longer book it is better to submit a book proposal.

A book proposal is a synopsis and two or three chapters. Many publishers insist upon this and specify their preference in their entry in *The Writer's Handbook*, which also gives editors' names and their address.

Always send the first three chapters, not chapters taken at random. It is no good thinking, 'This is a good bit, they'll like this.' They won't. They want to see the beginning to see how you hook the reader, how you display your characters and develop your opening situation. The synopsis tells them the rest of the story.

The synopsis and sample gets attention more quickly than a complete book and saves postage. Publishers can judge whether or not the book is of interest to them from this, and if they like what they see, will ask you to send the rest of the book.

It used to be considered bad form to send copies of your book to several different publishers at the same time, but nowadays this is no longer frowned upon. You can send your synopsis and sample to half a dozen publishers at a time. This is advantageous because publishers take a long time to consider MSS: three months is not an uncommon time to wait for a decision. The reason for this is that they receive a great many submissions which wait their turn from specialised readers. Then, a book which initially gets a good report may have as many as three readings by different members of the editorial staff before they make up their minds whether they want it or not.

If you have heard nothing after three months, it is in order to write a polite postcard asking if they have been able to come to a decision about your book, but be wary: nothing is more likely to ensure the rapid return of a MS than a pushy author.

Covering letter

The covering letter you send with your book proposal should be brief. Don't begin 'Dear Sir,' because 80% of the people in children's publishing are women. If you cannot find the editor's name in *The Writer's Handbook* telephone the switchboard and ask.

In this letter simply say that you are enclosing a book proposal and briefly explain why you think it will be suitable for their list, in terms of target age group, theme or central idea. See Figure 10 for an example. Be sure to mention the title of the book in the letter in case it gets separated from your MS.

Don't tell them your life story, but do mention any experience relevant to your writing. If, for instance, you are writing about gliding and you are a qualified glider pilot, it is useful to mention this. Whatever you do, don't praise your book to the skies or say how much your children/class, Aunt or Grandmother enjoyed it. You are not an advertising copywriter. Be low-key and businesslike.

The synopsis
This is not the outline, the scene by scene breakdown of your story that you wrote for yourself at the beginning. The synopsis should boil your book down to one or two pages and should be written in the present tense.

◆ Start with the title and say what the book is about, that is, the theme or central idea.
◆ Mention the target group at which it is aimed.
◆ Say who the main characters are and what they do in the story.
◆ Tell the story briefly, mentioning the high points.
◆ Round it off with the ending, showing how your characters have been changed by the events.

Query letter
In *The Writer's Handbook* you will notice that some publishers say they do not accept unsolicited submissions. If, however, you feel that this is the right publisher for

24th January, 200X.

Ms Polly Perkins
RAVEN BOOKS
110 Easy Street
London WC2

Dear Polly Perkins,

I have pleasure in sending you the first two chapters and
the synopsis of my fantasy story for 8-10 year olds called
THE MAGIC BICYCLE. It is based on the premise that every
1000th bicycle made is magic and tells of the adventures
of Tom who gets a magic bicycle for his tenth birthday. It
is 8,000 words and would, I think, fit into your Big Bird
series.

I was trained as a journalist and write occasional pieces
for magazines. I have two children aged 5 and 9. This is
my first children's book.

If you are interested I can send you the rest of the MS. I
look forward to hearing from you when you have had time to
consider this.

I enclose a label and stamps to cover return should this
not prove suitable for your list.

Yours sincerely,

Emma Payne.

Fig. 10. Model letter to publisher.

you, you can write a query letter briefly describing your book and any publication successes you may have had, asking if they would look at your MS. Be sure to enclose a s.a.e. for reply.

Sending off your MS

◆ Post it in a padded envelope and fasten with sellotape. Remember someone has to open this and hundreds of other packages. They don't want to do battle with dozens of staples and heavy-duty fastenings.

◆ Include a self-addressed label and either stamps or a cheque to cover return postage. You can make the cheque out to the publishers and leave the amount open, writing underneath, 'Not to exceed £5.00' (or just over whatever you think return will cost).

◆ Don't use recorded delivery or registered post because they make work. Keep a proof of posting slip (free from the Post Office) for yourself and enclose a self-addressed stamped postcard for the publisher to acknowledge receipt of your MS.

◆ Wait patiently and work on something else to keep you from biting your nails.

Rejection

This is something for which you must be prepared. It is rare for a novice to achieve success the first time out. This is where perseverence is all-important. Think of Bruce and the spider – if at first you don't succeed, try, try, try again.

Rejection by one publisher is not the end of the world, or of your book. The book may be perfectly sound but it has been rejected because there is something similar in the pipeline, or you may have chosen the wrong publisher. Publishers don't always have time to say why they are rejecting your MS.

Whatever you do, don't give up. Many famous children's writers suffered rejection before they were accepted – Beatrix Potter, Dr Seuss and Richard Adams among them.

Sometimes you get encouragement with a rejection. If an editor says something like, 'This one is not for us, but we would be pleased to see something else of yours,' this is real encouragement. This is not 'the soft answer that turneth away wrath'. They do not say this to people whose work they don't like. See sample rejection letters, Figures 11 and 12.

Acceptance

If a publisher decides to buy your book, an advance on royalties is usually offered. This means for each copy sold, you get a percentage of the price at which the publisher sells it to the bookseller, or on the cover price. It is important to find out which base they are using.

Do not sell *All the Rights* if you can possibly avoid it. This means you get one down payment and the publisher can sell your book wherever he wants in whatever form. He can sell film rights, TV rights and foreign rights without reference to you. All these rights are valuable, so check your contract. If in doubt contact the Society of Authors or the Writers' Guild, who will vet the contract if you join their organisation. (You become eligible for membership when you receive a book offer.)

Don't be taken in by vanity publishers who ask you to pay for publication. They will charge you a huge sum of money and will not distribute your book – that will be left to you, and you will find it hard to sell enough copies to recover the costs.

RAVEN BOOKS | CHILDREN'S PUBLISHERS
110 Easy Street, London, WC2. Tel: 020 7580 6768 Fax: 020 7580 6869

Ms. Emma Payne
Holly House
Ashen Market
Beds.

1st March 200X

Dear Emma Payne,

          THE MAGIC BICYCLE

Thank you for sending us your proposal for this book.
After careful consideration we regret to say this is not
quite right for us.

We are sorry not to write with better news, but wish you
luck in placing it with another publisher who may feel
differently about it.

Yours sincerely,

Polly Perkins

Polly Perkins,
Children's Editor.

Fig. 11. Sample rejection letter.

RAVEN BOOKS | **CHILDREN'S PUBLISHERS**
110 Easy Street, London, WC2. Tel: 020 7580 6768 Fax: 020 7580 6869

3rd March, 200X

Ms. Emma Payne
Holly House
Ashen Market
Beds.

Dear Emma Payne,

We enjoyed reading your book THE MAGIC BICYCLE. We are
sorry to say that we are not taking any more books for our
Big Bird series at the moment.

However, we like your style and if you would like to send
us something suitable for our Little Bird series for 5-7
year olds   1,500 words - we would be pleased to consider
it.

Your sincerely,

Polly Perkins

Polly Perkins
Childrens Editor

Raven Books is a Trademark® of Birdie Publishing House, 213 Rook Street, London, W1.

Fig. 12. Sample 'encouraging' rejection.

Self-publishing is an option, but it is too large a subject to
cover here. Read *Publishing a Book* by Robert Spicer in the
How To . . . series.

Some writers who do not want the expense of self-publishing choose to offer their book to an ebook publisher who, if he likes your book and thinks it is a commercial proposition, will consider taking your MS. This means your book will be sold from their site as a download that can be read on the buyer's computer or a handheld ebook reader. You will probably not sell as many copies as you would of a paper book, but the royalties are good – usually 45 or 50% of the selling price. To find out more, go to www.ebooksearchengine.com/ebooks/authors/resources/index.shtml

Do I need an agent?

New writers often think they will have more chance of getting their books published if they employ a literary agent. It is true that publishers give priority to MSS from agents whom they trust because agents do not take on work they do not think they can sell, so a submission from an agent has been through one sieve already. However, unless your book is right for them, publishers won't buy it just because it comes through an agent.

Getting an agent to represent you is difficult: they prefer not to take on anyone who has not already published something. If, however, you feel you need an agent, they are listed in *The Writer's Handbook*. Read the agents' fields of specialisation carefully to avoid wasting your time and theirs. Not all agents handle children's books.

The procedure for approaching an agent is the same as approaching a publisher: send a brief letter about yourself, a synopsis and two chapters plus return postage. Agents, too, take a long time to give a decision.

If you do get an agent, in return for offering your work to publishers, handling your contracts and haggling on your behalf, agents take 10% or 15% of your royalties and fees, and usually 20% on foreign rights.

What next?

As soon as your MS is sent out, do begin on your next project. You know now that you can write a book, so you will approach a new one with less trepidation than when you first started.

Go back to the earlier chapters of this book and begin plotting a new story. If you are lucky enough to get your first book published, your publisher will certainly want to see your next one and you will either have something ready to show him or you will be well on the way with it. Sometimes a second book succeeds while the first one failed, then with some alteration you can sell the first one.

Golden rules for submitting MSS

- Make sure what you are sending is as perfect as you can make it in terms of good writing, careful revision and immaculate presentation.
- Remember the three Ps, professionalism (be business-like), perseverance (keep on trying), and patience (be prepared for a long wait).
- Keep sending your MSS out. No publisher is going to call on you and say, 'Excuse me, have you a children's book we might look at?' As one of my students said to me, perseverance pays!

Books for Further Reading

Reference books

The Oxford Companion to Children's Literature, Humphrey Carpenter and Mari Pritchard (OUP, 1984). Biographical notes on authors and illustrators, book characters and plot summaries of important books.

Twentieth Century Children's Writers, edited by D.I. Kirkpatrick (Macmillan, 1978). Biographical notes on authors, bibliographies and critical essays on their work.

Grammar & words

Write Right, Jan Venolia (David St. John Thomas, 1986)
Modern English Usage, W.H. Fowler (Oxford)
Roget's Thesaurus, (Penguin, 1998)

Index of publishers etc.

The Writer's & Artist's Year Book, (A & C Black)
The Writer's Handbook, edited by Barry Turner (Macmillan)
For these two books, always use the current one.

Books about educational needs

National Curriculum for English:
  Books for Key Stages 1 & 2;
  Books for Key Stages 3 & 4 (Puffin)

The Puffin Literacy Hour Handbook, Wendy Cooling
The Waterstone's Guide to Books for the National Curriculum (Key Stages 1 & 2)

Aspects of writing for children

Inside Picture Books, Ellen Handler Spitz (Yale University Press, 1999)
The Art of Maurice Sendak, Selma Lanes (Bodley Head, 1980)
Writing for the Teenage Market, Ann de Gale (A & C Black, 1993)
Suitable for Children, Nicholas Tucker
The Cool Web, Meek, Wardlow and Barton
The Ordinary and the Fabulous, Elizabeth Cook
The Renaissance of Wonder, Marion Lochhead (Canongate, 1977)
Don't Tell the Grown-ups, Alison Lurie (Bloomsbury, 1990)
The Thorny Paradise, edited by Edward Blishen (Kestrel, 1975)
Children and Literature, edited by Virginia Haviland (Bodley Head, 1973)
Children and Fiction, Wallace Hildick (Evans, 1970)

Some of these books are out of print, so ask in your library.

Some more recent books

The Case of Peter Rabbit, Margaret MacKey (1998) (changing conditions of literature for children) available from Amazon.co.uk (£12.99).
The Fabulous Realm, Karen Patricia Smith (1993) (a literary/historical approach to British fantasy) available from Amazon.com but expensive ($62). Ask your library.

Best Book Guide for Children and Young Adults – 2003 edition available from Book Trust.

Children's Authors talk about the Craft, Creativity and Process of Writing, James Carter (1999) available from publishers Routledge Falmer (£13.99).

Sticks and Stones, Jack Zipes (2000) (The Troublesome Success of Children's Literature from Struwel Peter to Harry Potter) available from Amazon.co.uk (£15.99).

Children's Literature, Peter Hunt (2001) (children's literature from 18th to 21st century) available from Amazon.co.uk (£14.99).

Magazines for Writers

Writer's News, (monthly by subscription)

Writing Magazine, (bi-monthly) both obtainable from Victoria House, Ist floor, 143-145 The Headrow, Leeds LS1 5RL

The Bookseller (weekly, with twice yearly supplements listing forthcoming books)

The Children's Bookseller (appears in March and September) all from J. Whitaker & Sons, 12 Dyott Street, London WC1A 1DR

Mslexia by subscription from P.O. Box 656, Newcastle upon Tyne NE99 2RP

All these magazines are for writers in general, but do have items of particular interest for children's writers from time to time.

Books for Keeps (bi-monthly) 6, Brightfield Road, Lee, London SE12 8QF

Signal, Approaches to Children's Books (3 times a year) Thimble Press, Lockwood, Station Road, South Woodchester, Glos. GL5 5EQ

These are magazines reviewing children's books with articles of interest to children's writers.

Useful Addresses and Websites

Book Trust
Book House, 45 East Hill, London SW18 2QZ Tel: 020 8516 2977. Promotes Children's Book Week and has a comprehensive library of children's books.

Children's Book Circle
c/o Macmillan, 25 Eccleston Place, London SW1W 9NF. Tel: 020 7881 8000. Discussion forum for those involved with children's books. Monthly meetings addressed by invited speakers.

Scottish Book Trust
The Scottish Book Centre, Sandeman House, Trunks Close, 55 High Street, Edinburgh EH1 1SR. Tel: 0131 524 0160. Administers The Fidler Award for an unpublished novel for children 8–12 years old. Prize £1000 and publication by Hodder Children's Books.

The Society of Authors
84 Drayton Gardens, London SW10 9SB. Tel: 020 7373 6642.
Email: authorsoc@writers.org.uk

The Writers' Guild of Great Britain
15 Britannia Street, London WC1X 9JN. Tel: 020 7833 0777.
Email: admin@writersguild.org.uk
Website: www.writersguild.org.uk

Websites for children's writers
www.achuka.co.uk
> Children's books in UK. Frequently updated.

www.wordpool.co.uk
> Site for children's writers and for parents.

www.ukchildrensbooks.co.uk
> Directory of UK children's authors.

www.cbcbooks.org
> Children's Book Council.

www.scbwi.org
> Society of children's book writers and illustrators.

www.jbwb.co.uk/news.html
> A good site for news of markets.

www.underdown.org
> Purple Crayon – an American children's book editors' site.

www.write4kids.co
> An American children's writers site, but useful.

www.ucalgary.ca/~dkbrown
>   Children's literature web guide.

www.romeike.com/index.htm
>   List your chosen topic and this site delivers related press releases direct to your e-mail account free.

http://portico.bl.uk/
>   Online information service of the British Library.

This site is for children but could be useful for your research to find out what they are interested in.

http://groups.msm.com./TheChildrensBookWritersCafe/ cafecritique.msnw
>   Lists critique groups you can join.

www.bbc.co.uk/dna/h2g2/A425800
>   Helpful for creating fairy tales.

www.google.com
>   General search engine.

www.ebooksearchengine.com/ebooks/authors/resources/ index.shtml
>   Site for information on e-books.

Index

acceptance, 123
activity books, 104
agents, 126
alternative worlds, 19
animal stories, 20

beginnings, 67
biography, 103
book proposal, 101, 118
brainstorming, 43

card index, 44, 52
character checklist, 60
characters, 54, 108
coincidence, 80
complications, 49
conflict, 48
cutting, 106

description, 62, 84
dialogue, 63, 82, 109

ebooks, 126
emotion, 30, 31, 81, 87
ending, 90

fairy tales, 14, 42
families, 58
family stories, 24
first page checklist, 77

ghost stories, 26, 36

historical novels, 25, 37
horror stories, 26, 37

imaginary worlds, 15

joke books, 104

naming, 57
non-fiction, 97
notebooks, 9, 10, 43, 44

outline, 51–2

picture books, 28
plotting, 39
presentation of MSS, 113, 118,
    122
problem books, 25

reading, importance of, 6
rejection, dealing with, 122
rejection, reasons for, 4, 122
research, 4, 10, 24, 99
revising, 106
robots, 17
role-playing books, 17
rule of three, 81

scenes, 52, 80, 88

school stories, 24, 50
science fiction, 16, 19, 20
self-publishing, 125
series books, 32, 33
series books, lists of, 32, 100
settings, (see description)
Society of Authors, 123, 132
stand-alone fiction, 34
step-by-step books, 104
stimulus/response, 80
style, 68
synopses, 118, 120

theme, 53
thinking time, 8, 86
time-slip, 17
titles, 111

vanity publishers, 123
viewpoint, 69

word count, 116
writer's block, 86
Writer's Guild, 123, 133

young adults, 35